IN SEARCH OF
STEAM
PHOTOGRAPHING THE
WORLD'S STEAM RAILWAYS

KEITH STRICKLAND
FOREWORD BY CHRISTIAN WOLMAR

The History Press

Title page: First visited in 1982, China has long been a personal favourite destination for steam. Class QJ no. 921 waits for its next assignment at Fengtai marshalling yards in the south-western suburbs of Beijing in November 1982.

First published 2012

The History Press
The Mill, Brimscombe Port
Stroud, Gloucestershire, GL5 2QG
www.thehistorypress.co.uk

British Library Cataloguing in Publication Data.
A catalogue record for this book is available from the British
Library.

ISBN 978 0 7524 6560 9
Typesetting and origination by The History Press
Printed in Great Britain

Contents

Foreword
The Big Picture of Steam

by Christian Wolmar

The invention of the railways changed the world. Before the advent of the iron road, people's horizons were limited by the sheer difficulty of travel which made even a journey to the next village a rare event. In the space of a remarkably short period of time, the railways brought about a more radical transformation than had occurred since the dawn of man. As the railways shrank distance, they opened up unprecedented opportunities in virtually every aspect of life.

Within just a few decades of the inauguration of the first railway, the Liverpool & Manchester in 1830, the world was covered with their tracks and travelling hundreds of miles in a day, something that previously had been unheard of, became commonplace. The first few tentative lines were soon extended, and it was not long before it was possible to take a train from one end of Europe or America to the other. And while many technologies went into the construction of the railways ranging from rails and bogies to signalling and tunnelling, there was one that was at the heart of every railway until the end of the nineteenth century and, for the most part, far longer than that: the steam locomotive. Steam was the power that drove the Industrial Revolution and effectively enabled its spread across the world.

The concept of steam power had been around for more than a century when the difficult trick of putting it on wheels was achieved. Then there was no stopping it. The spread of the railways, enabled by the use of steam locomotives, changed everything. And I mean everything. It is almost impossible to think of an aspect of the early Victorians' life that was not changed by the advent of the railways. To cite just a couple, the very idea of bank holiday trips to the seaside was only made possible when coastal towns were connected to the rail network and the people brought back with them a taste for fish and chips, which thanks to the railway's ability to transport fresh fish, could easily be satisfied. Or, take the fact that until the establishment of big railway companies, a banking system to finance the provision of infrastructure was simply not available. The railways and capitalism grew together, a symbiotic partnership which historians have been unable, like the chicken and egg, to disentangle.

Keith Strickland's pictures fit very much into this bigger picture of the railways. Too many railways books, especially those which concentrate on photographs, have a narrow focus on the sheer power and beauty of steam. But they miss the point. Railways are important, and indeed attractive, precisely because of what they did for the world. They are not simply a piece of elegant technology, and that is why the steam locomotive needs to be celebrated and its images preserved.

These pictures do not concentrate on the technology or even, on many occasions, the locomotives themselves. Sure, they are ever present, but so is the context, whether it is a row of new sports cars that enable one to accurately date the picture, or the driver standing rather self-consciously and proprietorially by his magnificent engine. They are, of course, a celebration of steam, but not one enclosed within the narrow confines of the railway enthusiast, but rather demonstrating the wider context in which the steam locomotive operated. Of course, in among them, there are images that just reflect the majesty of steam, but it is almost always possible to identify a tell-tale sign of where and when the pictures were taken.

The author's preference for black and white helps situate the world he is portraying, not as a mere nostalgic throwback but rather as an enduring part of our heritage. The black and white photography, therefore, is a bonus. It's not only that we are missing nothing through its use, but quite the opposite. It adds to our appreciation of the images in these days when colour printing and reproduction is near universal but not always particularly revealing. Just as the history of steam should not be forgotten, neither should the importance of presenting a world where the nuances of black, white and grey provide all the information you need, leaving just enough for the imagination.

❖ ❖ ❖

CHRISTIAN WOLMAR is an author and broadcaster who has written a series of history books on the railways, including *Blood, Iron & Gold: How the Railways Transformed the World*. Since 1995 he has been a trustee of the Railway Children, a UK-based charity supporting street children who live on or around railway stations in many parts of the world, to which the royalties from the sale of this book are being donated.

The advent of steam trains overcame 'the sheer difficulty of travel . . . to the next village'. Burma, January 2007.

Introduction

Someone once wrote that voyages begin in books. If that's true, mine began with three. First came the *Ian Allan ABC of British Railways Locomotives*, the bible for every schoolboy train-spotter of my generation, which sparked a passion for looking at steam engines. Then one birthday or Christmas I was given the *Eagle Book of Trains*. This had pictures of railways at home and abroad. One in particular made an impression – a cut-away colour plate entitled 'an articulated locomotive' showing the innards of a South African Railways Garratt. Living in former GWR territory, I'd never seen anything like it and I couldn't imagine ever seeing one in the flesh. The English Lake District was the furthest I'd been from our Somerset home. Scotland was another world, let alone Africa. But the image stuck in the mind; and I still have the book.

Third, and quite a few years later, I picked up a secondhand copy of *Adieu Dampflok* ('farewell steam'), a superb photographic collection, mainly in monochrome, of steam at work in continental Europe. This really was the incentive to cross the Channel to savour everyday steam which by then had gone from BR – 'just once' I told my wife, but of course she knew better!

At the last count, my collection of steam photographs covered forty or so countries but in the early days I wasn't interested in the photographic side of things. There's virtually nothing from my train-spotting childhood. Even when I started to venture abroad a camera was no more than a means of making a basic record, first in black and white and later using colour negative film. It wasn't until the 1980s that a serious interest in photography developed with the acquisition of a decent camera and the setting up of a darkroom. This explains why previous books from my collection have not included material prior to 1981 and why, although this book starts with a picture taken in 1962, the quality of some of the earlier photos is less than one would wish.

As before, all of the photographs presented in this volume are in black and white, a medium which still appeals to me as being well suited to the steam railway scene. All have been taken on traditional (old-fashioned?) manual cameras though nowadays, after being developed professionally, negatives are scanned into a computer. The darkroom has been replaced by software.

This prompts a word about the ease with which a computerised image can be manipulated. Leaving aside the possibility of creating a wholly fictitious scene, there's a temptation for the person taking a picture to be lazy in composing the shot. That's a pity. Composition is surely one of the challenges of photography to be enjoyed. So is using a manual camera. Against this, one has to recognise the advantage which the software provides of being able to remove an unsightly feature which it was impossible to exclude from the original composition. Consequently a disturbing telegraph pole or the like has been excised from a few of the photographs in this book. Where such manipulation has had a significant impact on the image, this has been acknowledged in the caption.

While the sequence of photographs on the following pages is in roughly chronological order, the book is not intended to be a diary. Neither is the geographical coverage meant to be exhaustive. The choice of photographs has been influenced by personal preference and, in some cases, the stories behind the pictures. Two appeared in my first book published in 1991 and two have been used in magazines. Otherwise none has previously seen the light of day.

For the benefit of readers who like to know such things, I have quoted the makers' names and dates of construction of locomotives where ascertainable from standard texts, tour itineraries or, as a last resort, the web. The individual sources are too numerous to list. It is hoped that a blanket recognition will suffice. That said, acknowledgement is given particularly to the Continental Railway Circle whose publications are a mine of information and from whose *Journal* some quotations have been taken.

Thanks are due to Mike Arlett for proof reading the text, despite being a self-confessed Little Englander when it comes to railways, and for supplying the photograph on the rear dust jacket flap. The royalties from the sale of this book will be donated to the Railway Children, and I am particularly grateful to Christian Wolmar, a trustee of the charity, for contributing a foreword.

Finally, once more I must express huge thanks to my wife, Mary, for her encouragement and support. How many wives would agree to spend a New Year's Day chasing steam trains in India?

Keith Strickland,
Trowbridge, Wiltshire, May 2012

The constant procession of trains out of the open-cast pit at Sandaoling, in the far north-west of China, provides what many regard as the biggest steam show on earth today. In October 2011 class JS 2–8–2 no. 6261 storms the bank with a full load of coal bound for the washery.

I must have been twelve or so before I owned a camera – an Ilford Sporti if I remember correctly. With only two aperture settings 'sunny' and 'cloudy' and a choice of 'close-up' or 'view' for focusing, its technical abilities were limited to say the least. Moreover it had only one fixed shutter speed, probably 1/60th of a second, making it impossible to freeze a moving train. So it's not surprising there are very few photos of reasonable quality from my boyhood train-spotting days. By the late 1950s, the branch line from Taunton to Chard was a sleepy affair with few trains and seemingly little traffic. It was therefore no surprise when passenger services were withdrawn at the end of the summer timetable in September 1962. On the last but one day, school-friend Roderick poses while 0–6–0 pannier tank no. 8783 waits at Chard Central with the 3.15 p.m. train from Taunton. According to the public timetable, this train was due to arrive at 3.57 and to depart ten minutes later for Chard Junction.

1

The 1970s – Early Adventures

One of my most treasured and well-thumbed books as a small child was *The Modern World Book of Railways*. In it was a photograph of a most peculiar-looking locomotive. To my untutored eye this appeared to be two tank engines joined together back-to-back. The text told me that the loco belonged to the Festiniog [*sic*] Railway which had closed but whose engines could still be viewed in the line's locomotive sheds. For a Somerset boy, North Wales seemed remote and far away. Little did it occur to me that one day I would get there, let alone see one of these unusual locos in action. But so it came to pass during a summer holiday in 1962 with brother Malcolm and friend Peter. Though we rode the Talyllyn and Vale of Rheidol narrow gauge lines, it was the FR which caught the imagination and I have been a member of the Ffestiniog Railway Society ever since. More visits followed over the years and I suppose it wasn't much of a surprise that my wife and I spent our honeymoon near Harlech. Of course, by then I knew that the funny-looking engines were known as Double Fairlies. With an 0–4–4–0 wheel arrangement and two sets of cylinders on articulated bogies, they were designed for hauling heavy loads (by narrow gauge standards) uphill and around sharp curves. *Merddin Emrys* (below) waits to leave Portmadoc (since renamed Porthmadog) with a morning train for Dduallt in September 1971.

Adventurous is not a term which applied to me in the early 1970s. Until a holiday in France in 1972, I'd never been outside the UK despite reading geography at university. Starting married life, setting up home and embarking on a career left little time for chasing steam. Moreover because of the ban on mainline steam after British Railways' last steam train in 1968, opportunities were confined to preserved railways and the industrial scene.

Fortunately there was real steam not far from my Wiltshire home, just across the Somerset border. Kilmersdon Colliery was one of the last working pits in the North Somerset Coalfield. Production started in 1878 and continued until 1973. A short line ran from the pit-head to the top of an incline down which loaded coal wagons were lowered to the BR line at the foot. The cable incline was self-acting, i.e. the weight of the descending wagons was harnessed to haul up the empties. In 1929 the firm of Peckett & Co. of Bristol supplied an 0–4–0 saddle tank to work the line from the mine to the incline; and she continued to do so until the pit's closure. Now named *Kilmersdon* she has been given a home and a new lease of life by the Somerset & Dorset Railway Trust at their museum at Washford, Somerset, where she can occasionally be seen shunting. Today she looks a lot smarter than she ever did in the last days of the colliery.

The photograph below, taken in May 1971, includes the building which housed the winding gear at the top of the incline. A year later the loco rests between a spot of shunting (right). Part of the cable used to operate the incline can be seen in the foreground.

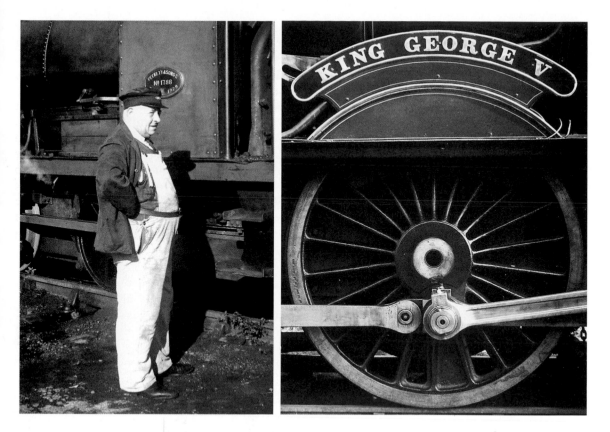

At the time of my visits, Herbie Loader was the regular driver at Kilmersdon. On the first occasion, I obtained a formal permit from the National Coal Board. I still have it. 'Don't bother with that in future,' said Herbie. 'Just come anytime.' So I did, sometimes taking my wife to ride with me on the footplate. On the last weekend of steam in September 1973, Herbie put on his best attire for the numerous well-wishers who came to say goodbye (above left).

As already mentioned, the powers-that-be banned steam on the national network after 1968. The famous GWR locomotive *King George V* was at that time kept at premises in Hereford belonging to Bulmer's Cider, visited on the way home from a weekend in North Wales in September 1971 (above right). A month later she was allowed out onto the mainline with a special train to Paddington. The success of this trial run encouraged a gradual relaxation of the ban to the point where steam on the mainline is now a regular occurrence enjoyed by enthusiasts, photographers and bystanders alike. Somehow, though, to me this isn't the real thing. Highly manicured pristine engines are not what I remember from the heyday of train-spotting in the 1950s. Chasing mainline steam specials in this country has never really had much of an appeal.

There matters might have rested had I not, on a whim, bought *Adieu Dampflok*, a photographic album of steam in France, Germany and Austria. This was my Damascene moment – the sudden realisation that everyday steam could still be found on the other side of the English Channel. By then steam on the SNCF, France's nationalised railways, had gone. So Austria and Germany it had to be. In the early 1970s there weren't too many organisations involved in arranging tours for overseas steam. One of the pioneers was To Europe For Steam (TEFS) and by good fortune it was advertising weekend trips to both countries in 1974, the first year of what has since proved to be a lifetime's hobby.

Austria came first – steam-hauled evening commuter trains out of Vienna, visits to two steam depots in the city, and full days on the famous Iron Mountain rack line and the narrow gauge Steyrtalbahn. Looking at my notes, I see that the total cost including flights and hotels was £38. I am also reminded that in the advance blurb participants were warned to take warm clothing. Rather obvious advice I thought for an Austrian winter. However it transpired that on an identical trip a year previously one member of the group had turned up wearing nothing more substantial than a sports jacket. After the first day in Vienna he was heard to remark that he hadn't seen a canal. He thought he'd been going to Venice.

Having always had a soft spot for narrow gauge steam, I was very taken with the Steyrtalbahn. This was a 760mm gauge line of some 25 miles in length though the last six were freight only. Connecting with standard gauge lines at both ends, it had a regular passenger service and carried extensive timber traffic. When the line closed in 1982, an 11-mile section south from the town of Steyr was acquired by a preservation group which runs trains in the summer and at holiday times such as Christmas. With a number of the original locomotives and rolling stock in use, the railway provides an authentic re-creation of the heyday of Austrian narrow gauge steam. Following the River Steyr for virtually the whole of its length, the line is also scenically attractive. The river is noted for its clear water, much favoured for nude bathing in the summer – apparently. Schubert often stayed at Steyr. The river is supposed to have provided inspiration for his 'Trout Quintet', though rumour had it that he spent a lot of time admiring the female swimmers.

Grey weather has accompanied all three of my visits to the Steyrtalbahn. 0–6–2T no. 298.25 is about to depart from the northern terminus at Garsten with the 13.15 train to Molln in February 1974 (left). Note the duffle bag – standard kit for train-spotting in those days. In October 2004, no. 298.53 (below) pauses at Sommerhubermuhle with a photographic charter from Steyr to Grunburg.

After the Austrian trip, I immediately booked for a weekend in what was then West Germany. Somewhat surprisingly in view of its rapid economic growth through the 1960s and '70s, the national railways still used steam to a considerable extent. One area which was easily accessible from the UK, being not far from the Dutch border, was the secondary mainline from Rheine to Emden. In the summer of 1974 this route was virtually 100 per cent steam with Pacific-hauled passenger trains and a substantial mineral traffic worked by 2–10–0s. It's true there wasn't much variety in the types of loco seen, even allowing for the occasional 2–8–2, but there was certainly quantity. Rheine shed had an allocation of 70+ engines, and a Sunday morning visit to the depot at Emden revealed over 40 – a sight for sore British eyes.

By now I had acquired a Zenith SLR camera and so was able to take moving trains with confidence. This proved fortuitous when some of the group decided to hire a couple of VW Beetles from a local garage to enable us to get to the railway line out in the countryside. Having

my driving licence on me, I found myself being volunteered to drive one of the cars. Ah well, there are far more hairy places for one's first experience of left-hand drive cars than Germany – as I was to discover years later on the dirt roads of Chile.

At Emden in August 1974, 2–8–2 no. 042 106-5 waits to leave with a train for Rheine (below) while in the opposite direction Pacific no. 012 075-8 has arrived with an express (right).

Less unexpected was the survival of mainline steam in the former East Germany throughout the 1970s and beyond. The German economic miracle did not extend to the Communist state. Moreover, the explosion of prices in the wake of the Middle East oil crisis in the early part of the decade led to some mothballed steam locos being returned to service.

Unlike those in many countries behind the Iron Curtain, the authorities in East Germany had a relatively relaxed attitude to railway photography. Enthusiasts were a fairly common sight, many from West Germany, so train photography tended not to attract the unwanted attention it did in other Eastern Bloc states. Exceptions were stations in border areas and anything connected with the military. Visas were of course required to get into the country and crossing Checkpoint Charlie in the middle of the night did not provide the most friendly of welcomes.

In the late 1970s Saalfeld, some 150 miles or so south-west of Berlin, was one of the main steam centres in the German Democratic Republic. The pride of the fleet were the oil-fired Pacifics used on the expresses to and from Leipzig where no. 01 0513-0 has just arrived at the city's main station in September 1978. Somebody told me off for using my camera here, but all was well. In fact, this was a group tour and we had an official permit for photography.

No. 41 1263-7 was a coal-burning 2–8–2.
She pauses at Quittelsdorf (above) in
September 1978 with a train from Erfurt to
Saalfeld. Earlier in the journey she passes
under a bridge near Singen (right).

For the steam photographer, Poland presented far more of a challenge than East Germany. The Communist regime seemed to regard railways in the same vein as military installations. No photography was allowed without a permit. Even then, if the local police chief didn't like the look of you or was just feeling grumpy, he or she could refuse to honour the official documentation. All of this was a great shame because at the beginning of the 1970s Poland had a dense network of lines and a huge number of steam locos, on both standard and narrow gauges. Most enthusiasts who ventured there did so in groups, partly on the safety in numbers principle and partly because a group was more likely to be successful in obtaining a formal permit than an individual. Once again, TEFS was something of a pioneer in this respect and so I joined a week's tour in September 1975.

Trying to land unsuccessfully in thick fog at Warsaw airport and a diversion to Copenhagen in a thunderstorm did not make for the best of starts. Later in the week, some members of the group experienced the inside of a Polish police station having been arrested for taking loco numbers. Elsewhere, the group was refused permission to visit the sheds despite a permit and a phone call to the relevant Government Ministry. We were put on the next train out of town and, to make sure we left, were accompanied to the first stop by guards and muzzled dogs. To add insult, back home I discovered that my camera had been afflicted by a bouncing shutter and nearly every negative was over-exposed down one side. This was definitely not the most successful of trips.

Even into the 1970s, Poland had an extensive network of narrow gauge lines on which ran a bewildering variety of loco types. No. 115, an 0–4–0 tender-tank, stands outside the small shed at Bialosliwie where the narrow gauge line from Wysoka met the standard gauge. These two places were only 5 miles apart as the crow flies, but the railway took 12 as it twisted and turned through the rolling countryside. I seem to remember there were no passengers apart from ourselves. No wonder the days of the narrow gauge were numbered.

If Poland felt adventurous with a hint of imagined danger, the perfect antidote was Switzerland, though it wasn't really on my wish list. By now the aim was to see as much of the world's real everyday steam trains as my bank balance and an understanding wife would allow; and Switzerland didn't fit the bill. But who could resist the temptation of a brewery with its own steam locos? Not me.

Rheinfelden is a small town on the Swiss bank of the River Rhine. Its two claims to local fame are its spa and the Feldschlosschen brewery which owned two steam locomotives to shunt wagons to and from the mainline, and which in 1976 was celebrating its centenary. In April that year, TEFS organised a group visit to the brewery where, after being steam-hauled by an 0–6–0 tank of 1907 vintage (above), we were given a guided tour before being invited into the tasting room and offered as much beer as we wanted. Since the beer was free, no one was impolite enough to refuse the accompanying cold white sausages.

The perils of roll film. It's not easy loading a new film on the hoof. Great concentration and a steady hand are required. Then there's the risk of dust or smuts getting into the camera while the back is open. Friend Ron (right) is determined to do things right during the course of a steam-hauled trip on the Sursee Triengen Bahn, a standard gauge branch linking the two Swiss towns in the railway's name. This was a memorable ride not so much because of the 1913-built steam loco pulling the train but because of the gourmet nature of the journey. At each successive station stop, a lunch course was served – hors d'oeuvres at the first, soup at the second, and so on – washed down with beer, of course.
My notes say the main course was goulash and Yorkshire pudding. Can that be right?

According to *Swiss Express*, the journal of the Swiss Railway Society, there is only one railway in Switzerland with the gauge of 760mm. Strange this, given that it was much favoured for narrow gauge lines in neighbouring Austria. The line concerned is the Waldenburgerbahn which runs from the mainline station of Liestal to Waldenburg. Essentially it is a roadside electric tramway, with street running in some of the villages through which it passes.

In April 1976, it was possible to charter a steam-hauled train using an 0–6–2 tank owned by a preservation organisation and acquired from the Steyrtalbahn in Austria. No. 298.14 has stopped in the square at Holstein (above) to pass a service train going in the opposite direction.

Switzerland has a well-deserved reputation for ensuring trains and buses connect. At Waldenburg (left), the postbus waits to take passengers from the steam special to their next destination.

Where next? Someone on the Swiss trip had been to India. Did I know there were huge numbers of steam locos still at work there? Hmm. Would I have the guts – literally as well as metaphorically – to go there? But as the journalist A.A. Gill once wrote: 'Of all the places you'll never get to because of squeamishness, trepidation, laziness and a dodgy bowel, India is by far and away your greatest loss.'

It's difficult to nail down the precise attraction of the country. The well-known tourist sights are only a fraction of the appeal. India is vast and has a huge variety of peoples, cultures and scenery to match. For the railway enthusiast of the 1970s, the big attraction was steam on four gauges – 5ft 6in ('broad'), metre, 2ft 6in and 2ft – with some 9,000 locos at the beginning of the decade, though diesels and electrification were beginning to make inroads. As the *Continental Railway Journal* put it at the time: 'India is the supreme Mecca for steam.' Remember, this was the 1970s when China was an unknown and unattainable destination. 'But rail travel can be extremely arduous physically and mentally exhausting. . . . Trains are often very crowded – so much so that it can be physically impossible to climb aboard – and huge contingents of people travel on the roof. In many rural areas foreigners are hardly ever seen and the appearance of an Englishman can attract a crowd in a matter of seconds which . . . will at best make photography impossible. In the cities the prevailing conditions under which the people live can be of such a desperate nature as to make railway photography appear somewhat irrelevant.'

First stop Bombay (now called Mumbai). What an eye-opener. Through recent TV programmes we have now seen pictures of the packed suburban trains, the people living in shacks on the side of the lines and the street children who end up living on or around railway stations. In 1977 one had only read about such things. Another sight which took some getting used to was that of women scavenging among ash for unburned pieces of coal as here at Lower Parel sheds, Bombay, in November 1977. From left to right are Class WP Pacific no. 7548 built by the Canadian Locomotive Company in Kingston, Ontario, in the mid-1950s, Class WG 2–8–2 no. 8844 constructed by the German firm Henschel in 1954, and Class AWD 2–8–2 no. 12650 built in the USA at the Baldwin Locomotive Works towards the end of the Second World War.

The 2ft 6in gauge Barsi Light Railway was owned and operated by a London-based company until purchased by the Indian Government in the early 1950s. It's therefore not surprising that the line's locos hailed from British manufacturers. The early morning train from Kurduvadi to Latur leaves Shendri in November 1977 hauled by Class G 4–6–4 no. 726. She was built in Manchester by the firm of Nasmyth Wilson & Co. in 1930.

Class F 2–8–2 no. 713 waits at Pangri to bank the train up the ghat to Ramling. Although hailing from the same builders as no. 726, she was four years older.

The Mysore Iron and Steel Co.'s plant at Bhadravati was one of the prime locations for industrial steam, having a fleet of locos on two gauges – metre and 2ft. Two narrow gauge 2–8–2s pose for photographers in November 1977. Both were built in Stafford, England, by W.G. Bagnall Ltd; the loco nearer the camera in 1957, the other in 1950. Bhadravati is nowhere near the city of Mysore. In fact, it was a five-hour bus journey to get there from our hotel in Mysore, and of course another five hours back. Roads and traffic are another part of the Indian experience. Of the return to Mysore, the official tour report talked of rushing 'beneath Banyan tress in the gathering darkness avoiding death on narrow lanes from approaching multi-coloured lorries and slow-moving bullock carts.' And when we arrived back at the hotel there had been a power cut. Even so, a bed in what had been the summer palace of a Maharajah was luxury compared to nights spent on a bunk of an Indian Railways carriage.

The metre gauge Class YL 2–6–2s were mixed traffic locos used on lightly laid branch lines. No. 5135 was being prepared at Mysore sheds (right) prior to working a passenger train to Nanjangud Town in November 1977. She was built by Henschel in 1956.

Birur is a junction on what in pre-Independence days was the metre gauge Mysore State Railway. The locomotive arriving with a goods train in November 1977, class YD 2–8–2 no. 30241, was originally from another of the former railway systems – the Bombay, Baroda and Central India Railway – and was built at that company's works at Ajmer in 1932.

YGs were the standard post-war 2–8–2 class on the metre gauge. Over 1,000 were built from 1949–72 mostly by Indian manufacturers but also Austrian, Japanese, and Czechoslovakian. Though the class was designed for freight traffic, no. 4387 pauses at Bolarum with an afternoon passenger train from Secunderabad to Medchal, November 1977. She was constructed by the Tata Engineering & Locomotive Company in 1959. The presence of photographers provoked plenty of curiosity.

The WP Pacifics were without doubt the most distinctive broad gauge steam class. No. 7724 (above) is on the ash-disposal road at Erode sheds, November 1977. Erode was and is an important station on the mainline from Chennai (formerly Madras) to Cochin in southern India, being the junction of a line to Tiruchchirappalli – Trichy in the days of the Raj. Pride of the fleet at Erode was sister loco no. 7723 (right). She had been decorated and burnished in preparation for a visit by a high-ranking railway official. In 1977 these two WPs were just eleven years old, having been constructed at the Chittaranjan Locomotive Works in West Bengal.

Looking back after 35 years and re-reading my notes, the amount of steam seen on that first visit to India seems incredible. The previous photographs only scratch the surface of what was there. But I was hooked and enthralled; and I knew one day I would have to return.

The Republic of South Africa in the apartheid era was described acidly by one railway author as a country where white men and black locomotives ruled. By the end of the 1970s it was obvious that steam was on the wane but a two-and-a-bit weeks' trip in 1979 produced 826 locos of 65 classes, according to the official report of the tour. True, this figure included some engines which were not in steam. That said, it's amazing now to think that such a remarkable haul was possible – and sobering to know it's unrepeatable.

Germiston was the main steam depot in the Johannesburg area. On a weekday there was a constant procession of locos leaving the sheds or returning from duty. No. 3810, seen in May 1979 (above), was a Class S1 0–8–0 loco designed for heavy shunting. Most South African Railways (SAR) steam locos were of British or German manufacture. This one was built by the North British Locomotive Co. of Glasgow in 1954.

Every steam shed on SAR seemed to have a favourite loco which was maintained in super-shine condition. At Germiston in May 1979 it was Class 12R 4–8–2 no. 1947 named *Rosie* (left). She was of 1920 vintage and hailed from the Baldwin Locomotive Works in America.

SAR's Class 25 and Class 25NC 4–8–4s were massive machines for a railway with a gauge of 3ft 6in. Many of the original 25s were built as condensing engines, a design in which exhaust steam was carried back to a very long tender and condensed into water. This enabled the locos to travel longer distances without the need to take on fresh supplies of water. However, the condensing equipment was said to be costly to maintain and the 25NCs were constructed without it, hence NC = 'non-condensing'. No. 3409 (above) was one of these. She was built by the North British Locomotive Co. in 1954. In May 1979 she leaves Sannaspos on the secondary mainline from Bloemfontein to Bethlehem with a wayside freight train – a 'pick-up goods' in British parlance.

Nearly all of the 25s were later converted to 25NCs. They were recognisable by the length of their tenders which made use of the frames of the former condensing units. No. 3459 (right) was photographed on the outskirts of Kimberley with what my notes say was the 8.35 a.m. train to De Aar, again in May 1979. At that time, the double-track mainline between Kimberley and De Aar was still 100 per cent steam and much photographed by enthusiasts.

Many South African mines used steam throughout the decade including some ancient classes of locos long gone from the national network. Loco no. 2 in the fleet at Apex Greenside colliery (above) was a survivor from 1905. With a 4–8–0 wheel arrangement, she was built in Glasgow for the then Natal Government Railways. No. 1 at the same location (below) wasn't quite so old. She was one of a class of ten 4–8–2s ordered by SAR shortly after its formation in 1910 and again delivered by the North British Locomotive Co. Both were photographed in May 1979.

Also in May 1979, Transvaal Navigation Colliery's no. 3 (above) heads a rake of loaded coal wagons to the exchange sidings with SAR; and a 4–8–2 tank loco (below) of British parentage rests between duties at Albion Colliery.

An industrial railway is not the most obvious place to find a Pacific, a loco designed for speed. This ex-SAR class 16CR was photographed in a sunny spot outside the running shed at Durban Navigation Colliery in June 1979. At the time of their construction by the North British Locomotive Company in 1919, these were the most powerful express passenger engines on the SAR. Lost glory, indeed.

In the late 1970s, one could still travel long distances on SAR behind steam. The daily passenger train from Cape Town to Port Elizabeth was a case in point, being steam-hauled for half of its journey of 42 hours. This trip involved two overnights. No problem, because SAR's first-class sleeping carriages put India's to shame. Moreover, the train had a proper dining car – in contrast to India where food was often ordered at one station and delivered at the next.

When I took this train in May 1979, the dining car was a 1908 vintage carriage (right) built in Britain and named *Palala*. The interior complete with fluted wooden pillars had an Edwardian elegance, matched by the faultless service. Even the china on the tables had been arranged so that the railway crest was facing the correct way. All in all, it was the perfect setting for enjoying good food and even better wine while listening to the sound of a steam locomotive hard at work at the front of the train – some people's idea of heaven.

Of course, one aspect of rail travel in the apartheid era was disagreeable and impossible to accept – the separation of 'white' and 'non-white' passengers, not just on the trains but also at stations even to the extent of separate footbridges. However, the magnificence of the locomotives and of South Africa's varied scenery meant a repeat visit was on the cards. Happily, when I went back in 1995 apartheid was history. Unhappily, so was everyday steam.

2

Onwards into the 1980s

Three weeks in South America in 1981 proved to be something of an endurance test. Four countries. Ten flights. Hire cars – night-time driving on unpaved roads. Language difficulties – why was an order of omelette and chips queried? Answer – the chips arrived inside the omelette. Strange local drinks – green Inca Cola anyone? Petty thieving in cities. Tropical rain. And always the unexpected – no petrol for sale on Sundays. But the railway interest made up for everything. Moreover, though we didn't realise it then, we were only just in time to catch everyday steam in Peru and on the narrow gauge in Brazil.

Until closure in 1983, there was a 2ft 6in gauge system some 250 miles or so to the north of Rio de Janeiro, known as the VFCO (Viação Férrea Centro-Oeste). At one point, the railway's route mileage exceeded 450 but by 1981 it had shrunk to about 130 based on the town of São João del Rei, the location of the works and main sheds. The big draw for the steam enthusiast was a fleet of Baldwin 4–4–0s, 2–8–0s and 4–6–0s. With their painted smokeboxes and polished brass they could truthfully be described as gorgeous. Nos 55 and 69, photographed at São João sheds in November 1981 (below), were 2–8–0s built in 1892 and 1894 respectively.

In November 1981 the *mixto* (mixed train) to Aureliano Mourão left São João at about 8 a.m. The timetable allowed five and half hours for a journey of 60 or so miles. There and back took all day. At 50p, a first class return ticket was good value. Part way through the outward run, no. 60 a 2–8–0 of 1893 vintage, takes water at Mestre Ventura. The jacks carried on the buffer beam weren't for decoration. They had been used earlier in the journey to re-rail the loco's front bogie after the train had hit a mudslide. The harsh tropical sun made for tricky lighting conditions photographically speaking.

In contrast to the rural charm of the VFCO, the Dona Teresa Cristina railway was an intensively worked coal-carrying metre gauge system south of São Paulo. In November 1981, no. 401 was marshalling wagons at Capivari washery. Bought second hand, she had been originally been supplied to Argentina by Skoda in 1949.

The start of the 1980s saw a developing interest in photography. Until then, a camera had been no more than a means of recording a few scenes on my travels. By 1981 the Zenith SLR had given way to the superior optics of a Pentax; and the spare bedroom which also housed a Hornby Dublo three-rail model railway became a darkroom. So began an attempt to do more than just point a camera and hope for the best.

Some of the most pleasing photographs result, perversely, from occasions when there has not been time to compose a shot. The picture above taken in December 1981 is an example. It's been published before but it's a personal favourite and I make no apology for using it again. As we drove up to the station of Padre Las Casas in southern Chile, the loco was just leaving. There was no time to do more than take a reading and press the shutter. The shot would have lost its impact had the boys realised they were being photographed and turned round to face the camera. The loco is an unidentified 2–6–0 and was captured leaving with a short freight train for Temuco on the 5ft 6in gauge mainline from Santiago to the south of the country.

At Temuco, one of the last steam strongholds in Chile, no. 488 (above) was the shed pilot in December 1981. She was an 0–6–0 tank built by Baldwin in 1907.

There's not much artistic merit in this photograph but the low evening sun made for perfect illumination of a scene which is now history. The grandly named standard gauge Ferrocarril Presidente Carlos Antonio Lopez in Paraguay seemed to be on its last legs in December 1981 though it struggled on for a while and makes another appearance in the next chapter. What made this railway fascinating was the fact that the loco fleet was 100 per cent steam and 100 per cent wood-burning. With no other trains on the line until the evening, the group I was with was able to charter its own special train for the day from the capital, Asunción, to the workshops at Sapucai and beyond to Tebicuary sugar mill where an ex-Buenos Aires steam tram loco was at work. The special is seen (above) at Ypacarai on the return journey. No. 237, a North British 4–6–0 of pre-First World War vintage, was originally supplied to Argentina. The coach was straight out of the Wild West.

It's easy to forget how difficult a country China was to visit and how little was known about its railways until the Communist regime began to permit limited tourism in the late 1970s. By 1982 the authorities had allowed in a few enthusiast groups but their itineraries were rigidly controlled. Vast tracts of the country were off-limits. Time spent at stations, sheds and by the side of the line was rationed so as not to miss the local silk farm or primary school. But the reports from these early tours spoke of huge numbers of steam locomotives and of new engines still being built. Add the chance to see some of the cultural sights and the appeal was irresistible.

'What was China like?' was everyone's question back home. Drab and regimented was the answer. But it was certainly different. Dog, rat or snake for dinner? No private cars. Streets thronged with bicycles. Everybody dressed in Chairman Mao suits. Chinese opera. The torso of a small child by the roadside. An abacus for counting money. Hand-drawn carts of night soil. Tip-up canvas seats on an internal flight. Yet looking back, it was a privilege to have been to China before the influence of capitalism and the impact of mass tourism.

Though construction of diesels was underway and some of the major routes had been electrified, steam predominated in many parts of China. Locomotives on the daytime passenger train from Datong to Taiyuan, a journey of some 230 miles, were changed at Shuozhou where in November 1982 class QJ no. 1355 backs onto the train.

The class QJ 2–10–2s were ubiquitous throughout China. Though intended for freight haulage as at Taiyuan (above), they were often used on passenger trains over steeply graded routes. One such was the line running north from Beijing to Badaling, a station adjacent to the section of the Great Wall most visited by tourists. In November 1982 there was at least one local stopping train to Badaling worked by QJs. As the precise location of the railway in relation to the road was unknown and as communication with the taxi driver was impossible except by sign language, photographing the train was a bit hit-and-miss. I'd like to be able to say the shot below was deliberately intended to be different. It wasn't. No. 893 was working hard against the gradient near Qinglongqiao. Another QJ was banking at the rear of the train.

Somewhat surprisingly, the locomotive factory at Datong was an approved tourist destination. At that time, China was proud of the fact that it was still building modern steam locos – the last country in the world to be doing so. That attitude was to change, for as the twenty-first century approached, the authorities seemed ashamed of what they regarded as an outdated and outmoded technology. In 1982 the factory built over 200 steam locos and employed 8,000 workers. With its own housing, hospital and five schools, it was a self-contained community. We were put up overnight in a workers' hostel, though the less said about the standard of plumbing the better.

Fresh from the paint shops, newly-built QJ no. 6376 stands outside the testing plant in November 1982.

Grab shots from the windows of moving trains are rarely successful. This one, taken from a Beijing to Datong passenger train in November 1982, is an exception. A very clean class JF 2–8–2 no. 2425 pauses at a wayside station with a freight train.

Tank engines were not at all common in China and mostly confined to industrial locations. No. 1018, a class GJ 0–6–0, was photographed at the entrance to engineering works at Nankou in November 1982.

The iron and steel works at Wuhan, a city situated on the River Yangtze, had a fleet of 60 steam locos. No. 219 was a class YJ 2–6–2. In the background is a class XK 0–6–0 no. 410. She was one of the many standard tank locos built in the USA and widely used in Europe during and after the Second World War. Apparently, twenty somehow ended up in China. It would be interesting to know how and why.

1985 saw a second visit to India. This time I knew something of what to expect and was prepared for the inevitable culture shock.

Lucknow achieved fame – or notoriety, depending on one's point of view – during the Indian Mutiny of 1857, now referred to in Indian history books as the First War of Independence, when British civilians and a handful of troops were holed up in the Residency. By the time the siege was lifted, many had died through disease or had been killed and the building was almost a ruin. As a memorial and a tribute to the dead, the Residency was never restored and, until the end of the Raj, the Union flag was never lowered at sunset. The ruins were thus the only place in the British Empire where the flag flew night and day – useful information for a pub quiz.

To enthusiasts in the 1980s, Lucknow was perhaps better known for its steam. By November 1985, locomotives were beginning to look less well cared for; and at the broad gauge sheds, class WP 4–6–2 no. 7617 had a decidedly grubby appearance. She was built in the mid-1950s by the Canadian Locomotive Company.

Lucknow also had a metre gauge shed where in November 1985 class YP 4–6–2 no. 2284 was photographed. This class was the standard post-Independence express passenger design for India's metre gauge network. 871 YPs were built, the first in 1949, the last in 1970. They came from four different manufacturers, no. 2284 being a product of the German firm Krauss Maffei.

Agra has long been a tourist destination, and justifiably so. As today's jargon would have it, the Taj Mahal is a must-see. A word of advice. Go there at dawn before the crowds arrive. Watch how the colour of the building changes as the sun comes up – assuming you have chosen a pollution-free morning. Magic.

Agra was another place with steam on broad and metre gauges. At one time, the 'Taj Express' from Delhi was worked by WPs. Now the mainline is electrified, though at the end of the 1990s the carriages remained of the traditional type with barred windows, about which my wife still has nightmares – but that's another story.

In November 1985 the group I was travelling with arrived via the metre gauge on the 5.45 a.m. Jaipur to Agra express hauled throughout its journey of five and a quarter hours and 150 miles by a YP Pacific. The train stopped at Bandikui Junction long enough to inspect YG 2–8–2 no. 3418 on an adjacent track. By now, readers will know that India's steam locomotives came from a wide range of manufacturers, at home and abroad. No. 3418 was built in India by Tata in 1962

I recall an on-time arrival at Agra. In India, as elsewhere, this was by no means a certainty. There's a story, perhaps apocryphal, of a gricer turning up at a station to catch one of the long-distance trains which criss-cross the sub-continent. Much to his surprise it arrived early. In fact, it was the previous day's train running 23 hours late.

After arrival at Agra Fort station, the stock of the express from Jaipur was shunted by no. 1538 (above). She was a class WD 2–8–2 built by the American Locomotive Company, Schenectady, USA, in 1943. There's a chap with a flag but that did nothing to deter people from wandering across and along the tracks. The scene is dominated by the Jama Masjid mosque, built in 1648.

Opposite, top: It wasn't just people who wandered everywhere with seemingly little regard for personal safety. In India cattle lead a charmed life. No. 1572 shunts empty carriages at Jaipur in November 1985. She was another class WD, though this time a 1948 product from the Baldwin Locomotive Works, Philadelphia. Pity about the pole emerging from the loco's chimney but the cows wouldn't stay still. Their construction details are unknown.

Opposite, bottom: As previously remarked, the local populace would often intrude into one's photography. Ekangar Sarai was a station on the 2ft 6in narrow gauge railway from Futwa to Islampur. How many of these good folk were railway staff and how many were onlookers? The loco was an 0–6–2 tank of 1919 vintage. Built by the Leeds firm of Manning Wardle & Co, she carried the number 1H. Why the suffix, I wonder? Class H, perhaps?

The Maharajah Scindia of Gwalior developed an extensive network of 2ft gauge lines in his state. He was also something of a railway enthusiast. In the palace's banqueting room there was a silver model train which ran around the dining table carrying after-dinner liqueurs. Moreover, according to one source, he was so fond of his steam locos that he built a mausoleum for one of them. That's taking one's love of railways a bit too far, methinks.

No. 759 was a 2–8–2 built in the USA by Baldwin in 1948. Seen in November 1985, she was being prepared for her day's work outside the sheds at Gwalior.

Next stop Pakistan. Another adventure. Outside of the main cities, there was a scarcity of hotels suitable for Western sensibilities. The solution for the tour operator was to charter a special train on which we ate and slept for ten days or so while we visited the country's remaining steam areas. The sleeping carriages proved to be more comfortable and cleaner than their Indian counterparts, though personal hygiene had the potential to be an issue. One's first shower (of sorts) was under a standpipe on a station platform. Meals on the train were excellent. Every day whenever the train stopped for any length of time, the cooks would disappear into the local market for fresh produce. Alcohol was forbidden and unavailable.

Surprisingly it was discovered that beer is brewed in Pakistan for consumption by visitors. So with a day to spare in Rawalpindi at the end of the tour, group participants took themselves to the former hill-station of Murree in the hope of finding the Murree Brewery. No such luck. After the premises were destroyed by fire a long time ago, the brewery moved to Rawalpindi; and by the time we got back there it was closed for the day. Ah well, Murree was a reminder of the days of the Raj when the governing class took to the hills in the hot season. The Anglican Church with its harmonium and *Ancient & Modern* hymnbooks would not have looked out of place in the Home Counties.

Among the British-built classes of locos still at work on Pakistan Railways in the 1980s, the class SPS 4–4–0s were the stars of the show. In the history of British steam, the inside cylinder 4–4–0 is one of the classic designs. No. 3002, photographed leaving Lala Musa with a passenger train for Malakwal in February 1988, was built by the Vulcan Foundry in Newton-le-Willows in 1917 for what was then the North Western Railway.

Almost without exception, the people we met in Pakistan were welcoming and eager to please. Children en masse were sometimes a challenge from a photographic point of view. All they wanted to do was crowd around and talk about cricket. The only difficulty encountered from officialdom was a nervousness about major bridges. Sadly, it seemed the occasional Brit still harboured colonial attitudes and an altercation at the River Indus near Hyderabad nearly caused an international incident. Generally, though, nothing was too much trouble and photographic run-pasts with the steam-hauled special train were readily arranged. No. 3005, another 1917 Vulcan product, was photographed en route to Malakwal where the bulk of the remaining SPSs were shedded. The smoke was to order. Since the country has no coal deposits, all of Pakistan's steam locos were oil-burners. Creating black smoke was just a matter of turning a knob.

Opposite, top: Also of obvious British origin were the class HGS 2–8–0s. No. 2277 was waiting to leave the yards at Samasata Junction with a freight train in February 1988. She too was built by Vulcan, this time in the early 1920s.

Opposite, bottom: From Samasata Junction a line ran east for 115 miles to Bahawalnagar over which our special train was hauled by a class CWD 2–8–2, no. 5085. Somewhere along the way, a photographic run-past was arranged with black smoke by request. Shortly after the picture was taken, herdsmen with camels wandered into view. It was a shame they hadn't arrived a fraction earlier as they would have added some local interest to the scene, always to be welcomed in my opinion. I have fond memories of this journey, sitting on the floor of an open doorway with my feet dangling over the edge, watching the life of rural Pakistan slip by.

No. 5085 was built by the Canadian Locomotive Co. in 1945. She waits to resume her journey after a run-past on the branch line from Bahawalnagar to Fort Abbas in February 1988. To meet a shortage of motive power during and immediately after the Second World War, 809 broad gauge 2–8–2s were delivered to India. Those built in the USA were designated class AWD; those in Canada CWD. Of the total, ninety-six went to Pakistan when the Indian sub-continent was partitioned in 1947.

Like India, Pakistan saw steam on broad, metre and narrow gauges. The metre gauge was a remnant of the pre-partition Jodhpur Railway. About 160 route miles ended up in Pakistan, based on the town of Mirpur Khas where two 2–8–2s were photographed (below) waiting to depart with local passenger trains in February 1988.

It was obvious by the late 1980s that the narrow gauge in Pakistan was not long for this world. From Mari Indus, a 2ft 6in gauge line ran 100 miles to Tank with a branch from Laki Marwat Junction to Bannu. A passenger train ran to Tank on Wednesdays, returning the next day. The rest of the system saw two trains each way each week. That was all. No. 203 was a class ZB 2–6–2 built in Hannover, Germany, in 1932. She was photographed at Laki Marwat shortly after arrival with the Thursday train from Tank. The railway ran near the tribal territories bordering Afghanistan, and the flat wagon in front of the loco was supposed to be some sort of anti-mine device.

There's another bus story attached to this photograph. Our special train had taken all day to travel from Mari Indus to Tank and it was nearly dark when we got there. As we didn't fancy an all-night journey back, our Pakistani guide found a local bus to take us. No matter that the driver had been hosing the bus with the windows wide open. Who minds damp seats? But as the evening wore on it became somewhat chilly. Those of us at the back noticed that the driver's door was open but so many freeloaders had crowded into the vehicle that we couldn't get down the aisle. A note was written and passed forward asking the driver to close his door. Some while later the note came back on which had been scribbled 'there is no door'.

It's impossible to cover all of the countries visited over the years. The Harz Mountains metre gauge system in the days of Communist East Germany appeared in my *Steam Railways Around the World*, as did Turkey and Peru. However, I can't resist including this photograph taken at Irmak, Turkey, in April 1984, because it depicts a class of locomotive familiar to UK enthusiasts. During the Second World War, twenty-five engines were ordered by Britain's War Department and shipped to Turkey to help alleviate a shortage of motive power. After the freighter carrying seven of them was sunk in the Mediterranean, two more were sent making a total of twenty which saw work in Turkey. Built by the North British Locomotive Company, they were the standard 2–8–0 design of the London Midland & Scottish Railway. Known to us as 8Fs, the local nickname for them was Churchills. At the end of 2010 two were repatriated to the UK though much repair work will be needed before they steam again. The loco in this photograph, no. 45161, was built in 1941. She is now on static display at the open-air railway museum at Camlik in Turkey.

The last major trip of the decade was to Zimbabwe. The country's second city, Bulawayo, was home to a fleet of Garratts used on routes north to Victoria Falls (the border with Zambia) and south to Plumtree (the border with Botswana). Using hired cars, it was easy to chase trains and, with perfect weather, this turned out to be an excellent trip from a photographic point of view. There was also an opportunity to ride the locomotives. A footplate journey of five hours through the African bush to Victoria Falls remains high in my personal top ten steam experiences. The falls themselves, visited on my birthday, were spectacular too – a day to remember. A goodly number of photographs of Garratts have featured in previous books of mine. Two must suffice here.

Marula is a station and passing loop on the single line to Plumtree. In July 1989, no. 424 heads towards Bulawayo with a freight train. She had a 4–6–4 + 4–6–4 wheel arrangement and was built by the Manchester firm of Beyer Peacock in 1950.

At the other end of the station, no. 420 makes a volcanic departure with the daily all-stations passenger train from Bulawayo to Plumtree. Look at that smoke! This engine was one of ten Garratts built in 1952 for Rhodesia Railways by the locomotive manufacturer Franco-Belge.

3

The 1990s
Steam in all Five Continents: Part 1

L et's start with America. The USA must have been a wonderful place for steam fans before the railroad companies succumbed to the smooth talk of diesel salesmen and before passenger traffic was decimated by mass car ownership and cheap air travel. Oil has a lot to answer for. Fortunately, there are books galore which give a flavour of the atmosphere of American steam railroads in their heyday. Even more fortunately, the USA has some superb heritage operations. Two of the best are situated in the Rocky Mountains in the states of Colorado and New Mexico. Spectacular is an overused word, but is a fully justified description of a journey on either of these lines. Both are remnants of the extensive 3ft gauge Denver and Rio Grande system. Built in the late nineteenth century to tap the mineral wealth in the mountains south and west of Denver, the railroad's last narrow gauge passenger train ran in 1951 though freight traffic continued into the 1960s.

For most of its 45 miles, the Durango and Silverton Railroad follows the Animas River, seen here in June 1990 as a backdrop to class K-36 2–8–2 no. 481 returning to Durango in the late afternoon with a train from Silverton. She was built by Baldwin in 1925.

There's no doubting the all-American appearance of class K-28 no. 473. She was one of a batch of ten 2–8–2s supplied by the American Locomotive Company (Alco) to the Rio Grande in 1923 at a time when the railroad was upgrading its narrow gauge routes. No. 473 was photographed in June 1990 approaching Rockwood with the first train of the day from Durango. Soon she will be on the section of the railway known as the High Line – a narrow shelf cut into the rock with a 400ft drop into the Animas Canyon below.

Opposite, top: The Cumbres and Toltec Railroad runs from Chama, New Mexico, to Antonio, Colorado, a distance of 64 miles. To reach the summit of the line at the Cumbres Pass, 10,015ft above sea level, trains have to tackle some fierce gradients. One of the steepest climbs is where the track runs through a cleft in the mountains, known as the Narrows. The gradient here is 1 in 25 (a 4 per cent grade in American parlance). In June 1990, class K-36 nos 488 and 489 burst out of the Narrows bound for the top of the pass.

Opposite, bottom: Class K-36 no. 484 rests outside the sheds at Chama after a day's exertions on the Cumbres and Toltec Railroad.

Much further north in the USA, the Conway Scenic Railroad is based at the town of North Conway in the state of New Hampshire. Once part of the Boston and Maine Railroad, passenger services struggled on until 1961, goods surviving another eleven years. In August 1994, 0–6–0 no. 7470 was the resident steam locomotive, photographed on the turntable outside the small roundhouse. She was built in 1921 in Montreal, Canada, at the workshops of the Grand Trunk Railroad.

Inside the roundhouse at North Conway. We in the UK tend to forget the importance of a powerful headlight in countries where railway tracks are often unfenced.

1992 saw a return to South America on a two-week tour, the highlight of which was the Esquel branch of what was once the Ferrocarril General Roca in Argentina. With a gauge of 750mm, this line ran 250 miles from Ingeniero Jacobacci, a junction with the broad gauge, to Esquel. To say the train service was sparse would be an understatement. In 1992, the one mixed passenger and freight train (*mixto* in Spanish) ran one way on Fridays and the other on Saturdays. Miss it and there'd be a whole week to wait for the next one.

And miss it we nearly did. Flying late into Buenos Aires, we only just made our connection with the last plane of the day to Bariloche in Argentina's lake district. From there it was a night-time bus ride over atrocious dirt roads to Ingeniero Jacobacci. Checking in at the one-horse town's only hotel at 4.00 a.m., we were up again an hour later to catch that Friday's train. Was it worth it? Of course. The last few pages of Paul Theroux's *The Old Patagonian Express* convey the remoteness and desolation of this part of the world and the decrepitude of the train: 'It was a steam train . . . a kind of demented samovar on wheels, with iron patches on its boiler and leaking pipes on its underside and dribbling valves . . . it made such a racket of bumping couplings and rattling windows and groaning wood . . .'

In December 1992, the Friday train from Ingeniero Jacobacci was photographed near Cerro Mesa double-headed by two 2–8–2s built by Baldwin in 1922. The leading loco is no. 16.

Saturday's return train leaves Norquinco. Wow!

It's pub quiz time again. Where is the most southerly railway in the world? Since 1994 it's been a small tourist railway at Ushuaia, Tierra del Fuego, which markets itself as the railway at the end of the world. Prior to that it was a 750mm gauge line built to carry coal from mines at Rio Turbio to the port of Rio Gallegos 160 miles away. The railway operated a fleet of 2–10–2s built in Japan by Mitsubishi in 1956 and 1963, some of which were photographed at the sheds at Rio Gallegos in December 1992 (below). In addition to its port, Rio Gallegos had a major military base used by the Argentinian air force during the Falklands War. We were warned not to wear Union Jack t-shirts. Yet we had dinner in the wood-panelled dining room of the *Club Britanico,* a gentlemen's club for the owners of the cattle ranches in the area many of whom dressed in the style of an English country squire, reflecting the fact that much of the population is descended from European settlers. Talking of beef, nowhere have I eaten more succulent – or larger – steaks than in Argentina. It's not a country for vegetarians.

Can there be another person in my home town who has been to Paraguay not once but twice? This is not a boast. It's one of the poorest countries in South America and has no obvious tourist attractions. Who would want to go there? My second visit in December 1992 was anything but smooth. A cancelled flight meant a long bus journey to get to the capital, Asunción, only for the one passenger train of the day to derail itself before we had had an opportunity to photograph it. Two days later, the loco hauling our special train on the Abai branch ran out of water near José Fassardi (below). That was the end of that journey. While waiting for the rescue bus, we had ample opportunity to photograph the disgraced loco, 2–6–0 no. 59. It was dark by the time the bus arrived and there were more than a few hours of dirt roads to negotiate before we reached bed. By then we didn't care when and by whom no. 59 had been built. For the record, it was 1910 by the North British Locomotive Co. Note what the wagon behind the engine was carrying. Paraguayan locos burned wood. The result of riding on the open balcony of the carriages was a shirt full of holes.

Heath Robinson would have loved the Ferrocarril Presidente Carlos Antonio Lopez. Even the name has a touch of Ruritania about it. Now it's all gone, seemingly abandoned.

Right: No wonder trains were derailed. Just look at the track in this photograph taken near Asunción's botanical gardens in December 1992. The rails (of standard gauge) appear to have been laid directly on the ground without any ballast. No. 102 was another North British 2–6–0 of 1910 vintage. The buffers on Paraguayan locos were hinged so that they could be swung upwards. This odd arrangement was designed to minimise damage to any object which a locomotive might unwittingly hit while working in a chimney-first direction. Presumably animals were the most likely obstruction to be encountered.

The American continent in the guise of the Caribbean's largest island, Cuba, appears again in later chapters. Meanwhile, I made my one and only visit to New Zealand in 1991. Now that's a civilised place to enjoy railways – familiar food, excellent wines and old-fashioned (in the best sense of the term) courtesy and hospitality. It's many a day since steam on the country's railways was an everyday occurrence. However, there's a strong heritage movement reflected by a number of photographs in my *Steam Through Five Continents* and I can't resist one more of class Ab Pacific no. 778 departing from Kingston, South Island. Built in the New Zealand Railway's own workshops in 1925 to a gauge of 3ft 6in, this to my eyes is a most handsome machine. Burnished and polished, she was a magnificent sight. Six of us were able to charter her and her train, known as the 'Kingston Flyer', for a morning's photography with yours truly riding in the spotless cab. This may not have been the most heart-stopping steam experience but it was certainly a great deal of fun. Sadly, at the time of writing, the future of this particular steam operation appears to be in doubt.

After the fall of Communism, railway photography in Eastern Europe became less hazardous. Though it took a while for some of the old bureaucratic attitudes to disappear, the authorities generally adopted a more relaxed approach towards enthusiasts. Nowhere was this change more evident than in Poland. In April 1994 the Steam Railway magazine ran a 48-hour trip to sample Polish standard and narrow gauge steam. Here was a chance to see how much things had changed from the bad old days.

At the time, Wolsztyn was at the hub of five routes though two saw only freight trains. Arriving at the sheds before dawn for a session of night photography, we were given unrestricted access. No men with guns. No muzzled dogs. No awkward questions. Quite the reverse. Everyone seemed pleased to see us.

The oldest active loco was a class Ok1 no. 359 built at the Schwarzkopf factory in Berlin in 1919. She was steamed specially for the visit and was photographed at the sheds prior to working the 11.05 passenger train to Poznan. As recounted in a previous chapter, this was a pre-First World War design which survived into the 1970s not only in Germany but in other parts of Europe which had been overrun by the German armies in the Second World War. Though the class was still common when I visited Poland in 1975, by 1994 no. 359 was the country's sole working example.

Class Ty3 no. 2 was another German loco which was absorbed into Polish stock after the Second World War. Built during the war, she was a heavier version of the standard 2–10–0 *kriegslokomotiven* (war locomotives). She heads a mixed train from Wolsztyn to Konotop in April 1994.

In Ukraine, an enterprising entrepreneur acquired a complete train of coaches which he hired out to photographic groups from the West. One such group chartered the train in September 1994 for a week's travel using a number of different steam locos. As the train included sleeping cars and a restaurant car, we lived on it for the whole week. Nothing seemed too much trouble. The crew knew what we wanted in terms of photograph locations and run-pasts. They had also cottoned on quickly to the ways of capitalism. A cabside plate incorporating the hammer and sickle emblem of the USSR was sold for a few dollars and transferred to my ownership.

Before setting out the group had been given a guided tour of Kiev. This included the Orthodox Cathedral where a service was in progress. I mention this only because of the sublime and (to me) spine-tingling choral music. Somewhere there's a thesis waiting to be written on the connection between railways and music – more specifically church music.

The class Su (Cy in the Cyrillic alphabet) 2–6–2s were an improved version of a pre-Revolution design which originated at Sormovo works (hence class S). The suffix 'u' derives from *usilenny*, which translates as strengthened. Used on all but the heaviest passenger trains, so successful were these locos that some 3,700 of this class and its predecessor were built between 1910 and 1951. No. 251-86 performs a run-past for the photographers between Grechany and Krasilov. Ukrainian railways run on tracks with the Russian gauge of 5ft.

No. 251-86 waits for the green light at Novograd Volynsky.

Class SO (CO in the Cyrillic alphabet) was named after Sergo Ordzhonikidze who was a close friend of Stalin. Almost 2,000 of this class were built between 1935 and 1941. With a 2–10–0 wheel arrangement, they were intended for freight traffic. No. 17-4371 was photographed near Pukov en route to Berezovitza.

No. 17-4371 makes a splendid sight as she departs Berezovitza. The second locomotive is class L no. 5141. This class was a post-Second World War 2–10–0 heavy freight design. The dumped goods wagons to the left are a reminder of a visit to the sheds at Korosten to see a rare tank locomotive at work. Stored there were condemned coaches which had been taken out of service because of the fear of contamination from Chernobyl. Scary.

In the Communist era, new classes of locomotives were often named after people. Class L seen on the previous page was a reference to its designer, one Mr Lebedyanski. Class FD was so named in honour, if that is the right word, of Felix Dzerzhinsky, the founder of the Soviet secret service. More than 3,000 FDs were built in the ten years from 1931. They too were freight engines, having a 2–10–2 wheel arrangement. No. 20-2714 puts on a show (above) for the photographers between Larmolintzy and Kadievka . . .

. . . and, above, en route from Kamenez-
Podolsky to Larmolintzy.

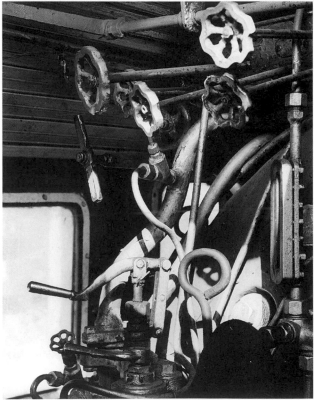

A corner of no. 20-2714's cab.
Goodness knows what all the knobs and
levers are for.

Visually, the class P36 4–8–4s were the most impressive steam locomotives built in the USSR. Designed for express passenger work, about 250 of these locos were constructed at Kolomna locomotive factory south-east of Moscow between 1954 and 1956. Most of the class carried the normal passenger livery of light green and red wheels with white rims, but a few were in blue. 'Once seen, never forgotten' is an apt phrase. No. 0050 pauses at Zhitomir. The class letter P derives from the Russian *pobyeda*, meaning victory.

Apart from a footplate ride on this magnificent machine, what else do I remember about Ukraine? First, never to refer to the country as *the* Ukraine. The people hate it. Second, local 'champagne' is best avoided if one wants a clear head in the morning. Third, not everyone saw the fall of Communism as a universally good thing. As in other former Eastern Bloc countries, the withdrawal of state subsidies caused many industries and factories to go to the wall. Not only did this leave many people without a job, it also led to a decline in the amount of freight traffic on the railways – hence all those laid-up goods wagons. At the same time, the abrupt transition to a market economy was accompanied by inflation, and former state employees on fixed pensions saw the real value of their income fall dramatically. Others of course welcomed the change, not least the entrepreneur with his special train even though he had a rude introduction to capitalism when one of the first UK groups to charter the train went bankrupt and couldn't pay the bill.

From one photographic safari to another – South Africa. Steam finished on South African Railways in the early 1990s. Fortunately, the authorities were willing to cooperate with charter groups by providing locos and stock to re-create scenes from the steam era. The Drakensberg Farewell Railtour was organised by the UK operator Steam & Safaris and in July 1995 ran for two weeks, starting at Bloemfontein and ending at Cape Town. Once more, the train was home for the whole of the time. The absence of charming Ukrainian waitresses in national costume was more than compensated for by the standard of on-board catering. The cuisine was just as good as I had remembered from 1979, as was the wine.

If I had to choose the top three group tours I've been on, the Drakensberg Farewell Railtour would be one of them. (The other two would be Hungary and Burma, both of which appear in later chapters.) The combination of magnificent scenery, just the right weather – warm but not so warm as to preclude photogenic steam effects – and nigh-on 200 run-pasts or false starts meant a very successful trip from a photographic point of view. Some twenty photographs were used in my last book, *Worldwide Steam Railways*. More appear here.

Class 19D 4–8–2 no. 3323 catches the evening sun as she rounds a curve on the Barkly East branch. She was built by the North British Locomotive Co. in 1948.

Sister loco no. 2698 was photographed at Dempsey on the Maclear branch. Most but not all South African locos were purchased from British or German manufacturers. No. 2698 came from the Berlin firm of Borsig just before the outbreak of the Second World War. The 19Ds were the second most numerous class on South African Railways (SAR), numbering 235. They were used extensively throughout the network on secondary routes hauling both passenger and freight trains.

No. 2698 again, this time near Birds River with a train from Indwe to Sterkstroom. The coach at the rear was for the photographers. This may be the point at which to explain to the general reader what are run-pasts and false starts. The latter involves the photographers positioning themselves in order to take a picture of the train departing from a station. Once the train has passed the group, it stops and everyone walks forward to board it.

A run-past needs a little more organisation. First, someone – usually the group leader – selects a location and asks the driver to stop. Those wishing to take a photograph then get off the train, carefully, and take up positions making sure no one gets in each other's way. The train reverses, preferably until out of sight, before running forward past the assembled company. Having stopped ahead, the driver may back the train to enable the group to reboard. Otherwise, it's a walk forward. Easy? Not really. Photographers are a hard bunch to please. Is the sun out? Will the engine be working hard enough? Will there be black smoke? If so, which way is the wind blowing? No wonder master shots are few and far between.

The aftermath of a false start at Priors station. Wire fences can be a bit of a nuisance.

No. 3410 *Paula* makes a splendid sight near De Brug with a train on the secondary mainline from Kimberly to Bloemfontein. This is a scene to savour. All the ingredients were right – a low sun, a cloudless sky and plenty of black smoke lifting clear of the train. Even the poles and wires could be used to good effect as a frame for the picture. All that's missing is the sound. There were many smiling faces among those getting back on the train. It was time for a drink in the bar car.

The inclusion of this photograph gives an opportunity to correct an error in the text of *Worldwide Steam Railways* where this loco is quoted as having a 2–10–2 wheel arrangement. Built by the North British Locomotive Co. in the early 1950s, no. 3410 is in fact a class 25NC 4–8–4.

Paula again, between Drieklof and Oliehoutplaat. Further comment seems superfluous.

In the South African winter, early morning often provided excellent conditions for steam photography. Class GO Garratt no. 2575 thrilled the photographers with this run-past between Mission and De Vlei on the line from Caledon to Cape Town. With a 4–8–2 + 2–8–4 wheel arrangement, no. 2575 was supplied to SAR by the German firm Henschel in 1954.

Class GMAM Garratt no. 4072 was another Henschel product of the early 1950s. In a re-creation of the days when the daily Cape Town to Port Elizabeth train was steam-hauled over the Montagu Pass, she emerges from one of the tunnels on the southern side of the pass. This is another photograph which would benefit from sound accompaniment.

In 1979 this old-timer was mounted on a plinth at Kimberley railway station. By 1995 it had been restored and saw occasional use on special trains. Built by Neilson Reid & Company of Glasgow in 1902 for the then Cape Government Railways, no. 645 was a Class 6J 4–6–0. In their day, these locos worked the crack expresses between Cape Town and Johannesburg. Neilson Reid merged with the companies Dübs and Sharp Stewart in 1903 to form the North British Locomotive Company. At one time the largest loco-manufacturing enterprise in Europe, this company exported engines throughout the British Empire as is apparent from many of the photographs in this book.

No. 645 was photographed leaving Kimberley with a train for Perdeberg. A cloudless sky and a nip in the air made for great steam effects.

4

A Miscellany
and an English Interlude

France once had an extensive network of minor railways, *secondaires*, criss-crossing the country. I think I read somewhere that it was once possible to travel from the top to the bottom of the country by a succession of trains using nothing but these minor lines, though I suspect this may be the French equivalent of an urban myth. If true, it would have taken weeks to accomplish, for the *secondaires* were built to serve the needs of local communities and many were of narrow gauge. Most of these lines found it impossible to compete against the motor car and bus, and few survived into the 1960s. Fortunately, one or two lasted long enough to be given a new lease of life in the preservation era.

With its headquarters at St Valery from where William the Conqueror is supposed to have sailed, the *Chemin de Fer de la Baie de Somme* (CFBS) operates trains over 14 miles of metre gauge track. This delightful railway is very accessible by car from the UK via the Channel Tunnel, and my wife and I have spent many a long weekend in the area.

In July 1998, 2–6–0 tank locomotive no. 1 *Aisne* stands on the quay at St Valery with a train for Noyelles. She was built by the firm of Corpet-Louvet in 1906 and originally worked in the French *département* after which she is named.

No. 1 was later photographed arriving at Noyelles. This is where the CFBS meets the main railway line from Boulogne to Paris. From here to the quay at St Valery the track is of mixed gauge, the standard gauge rails straddling the metre pair. In times gone by this enabled goods to be carried in standard gauge wagons, thus avoiding the need for transshipment at Noyelles. The CFBS is twinned with the Kent & East Sussex Railway and the standard gauge occasionally plays host to a visiting loco from England. The Triumph sports cars were visitors of a very different mode of transport.

To ring the changes, here's a selection of bits and pieces seen during four decades of chasing world steam.

Far left: An old level-crossing warning sign of obvious British origin seen in Sri Lanka in February 1994.

Above: The cabside numberplate of a metre gauge class YG 2–8–2 photographed at Delhi in December 1998. The brass plate from sister loco no. 3345 is in my collection though it's far less elaborate.

Centre: A travelling post box, New Zealand, October 1991.

Right: The station sign at Galera is proof of a visit to Peru in December 1981. Until China opened its railway to Tibet in the twenty-first century, this was the highest point reached by a passenger train anywhere in the world.

Above: Exhortations to the workforce were frequently seen at Indian sheds. Mostly they were about safety or coal consumption. This one photographed in November 1977 was rather different.

Left: Seen on the back of a t-shirt in Serbia in June 2008. The carriages of the Romantika museum train are used for steam-hauled charters.

Without the company of people, travel would be a dull affair.

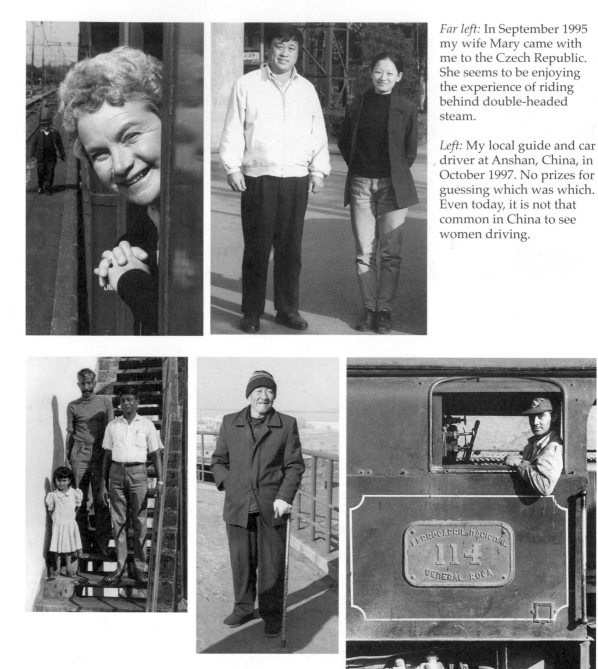

Far left: In September 1995 my wife Mary came with me to the Czech Republic. She seems to be enjoying the experience of riding behind double-headed steam.

Left: My local guide and car driver at Anshan, China, in October 1997. No prizes for guessing which was which. Even today, it is not that common in China to see women driving.

Above, left: Signalmen and family at Hatton, Sri Lanka, photographed in February 1994.

Above, centre: On a footbridge spanning the coal railway at Beipiao, China, this elderly gentleman was curious at meeting two westerners in November 2009.

Right: A driver on the Esquel line, Argentina, December 1992.

Sometimes one comes across the strangest things. On a sunny morning in July 1995, the Drakensberg Farewell Railtour was happily bowling along the branch line from Springfontein to Fauresmith, South Africa, when the train came to a sudden halt. Ahead was the surprising sight of a van straddling the rails. It appears the driver was taking a short-cut having believed there to be no trains about. The only way of clearing the track was to manhandle the van to one side. I pleaded a dodgy back.

The only diesel to be seen in this book, appropriately in a state of disgrace (above). In March 1995 the Eduardo Garcia Lavandero *central* (sugar mill) in Cuba had at least one loco in steam. There was also this diesel shunting the mill yard. Waving and smiling from his cab to impress the watching visitors, its driver set off with a rake of wagons at a cracking pace. Crash. Bang. The diesel had split the points. Now it was the spectators who were smiling. Another happy chap was the sculpted panda (above right) guarding a level crossing on the Pingzhuang coal railway, China, in October 2011. Bizarre.

The next seven photographs represent an unashamed plug for the West Somerset Railway (WSR). There's no apology for the fact that all were taken at familiar locations and that all depict locos of Great Western Railway (GWR) ancestry. They are included because I like them.

In my childhood, I knew the line from Taunton to Minehead very well. Living in Taunton and having no car, my parents used the train for family outings to the seaside. Later the branch was a way of reaching Exmoor for a day's hiking with a girlfriend – now happily my wife.

Though having moved away from Somerset by then, I was sad when BR closed the line at the beginning of 1971. When it reopened three years later, I felt the least I could do was to buy a few shares in the company. Never did I think that the railway would become the thriving and successful enterprise which it is today. One of the major heritage railways in the UK, it makes a significant contribution to the local economy as well as giving considerable pleasure to enthusiasts and the travelling public alike.

No. 7828 *Odney Manor* runs round its train at Bishops Lydeard in August 1995. The Manors were designed for use on secondary mainlines. No. 7828 was the penultimate member of the class, emerging from Swindon works in 1950 by which time the GWR was no more. In 2011, she carried the name *Norton Manor* in honour of '40 Commandos' whose camp near Norton Fitzwarren is adjacent to the WSR.

No. 7820 *Dinmore Manor* was photographed at Watersmeet with a late afternoon train for Minehead in March 1997. She too was built at Swindon in 1950. The former GWR lines in West Wales were some of the last stamping grounds of the Manors; and Shrewsbury was the final shed of nos 7820 and 7828 prior to their withdrawal in 1965. The tree at the left of this scene has been described as the most photographed walnut tree in England, such is the popularity of this spot, a mile or so north of Bishops Lydeard station, with lineside photographers.

In common with many other heritage railways, the WSR attracts visiting locomotives. Among former GWR classes, Kings and Castles have appeared; but to me they look out of place on what is essentially a country branch line. Though they never worked on the Minehead branch in years gone by, Manors and Halls just about look right because of their more modest size. Ah well, one can't please all of the people all of the time, and visiting stars certainly pull in the punters.

In 1997, no. 4920 *Dumbleton Hall* spent some time on the WSR. She was photographed at Nethercott Bridge, another favourite location between Bishops Lydeard and Crowcombe Heathfield, with a morning train to Minehead in March of that year. No. 4920 was built at Swindon in 1929 and withdrawn in 1965. Talking of things not looking right, I must point out the ex-diesel multiple unit trailer coach immediately behind the loco. Ugh. On a happier note, I think the birds circling overhead were buzzards.

From Bishops Lydeard, the current starting point for trains to Minehead, it is a continuous climb to the summit of the line at Crowcombe Heathfield. 0–6–0 pannier tank no. 7760, a visitor to the railway, was going well when she was photographed at Nornvis Bridge in March 1997. Used for shunting and on light goods or passenger trains, these tank engines could be found in every corner of the former GWR network. It is sad that the WSR doesn't have one on a permanent basis.

Taunton was one of those places where the sound of steam locos shunting could be heard all night. We lived within earshot of the railway. On still summer evenings with the windows wide open, I used to be lulled to sleep by the comings and goings of locos at work in the goods yards. My very first footplate ride at the age of six was, courtesy of a friendly driver, on a pannier tank. One tends to think all GWR locomotives were built in the company's own workshops. Not so. Outside firms were used when the railway's works had no spare capacity. No. 7760 is a case in point having been constructed by the North British Locomotive Co. in 1930. After withdrawal by BR in 1961, she was purchased by London Transport, renumbered L90 and used for about nine years on maintenance trains.

Crowcombe Heathfield – a quintessential English country station and a personal favourite. With only a few houses nearby, it is in the depths of the Somerset countryside. In the gaps between trains, peace reigns. As a schoolboy, I didn't dream for one minute that fifty years later I would be a volunteer signalman here.

No. 4160 arrives with an afternoon train from Bishops Lydeard in August 1995. She looks every inch a GWR thoroughbred, but in fact emerged from Swindon works in September 1948, nine months after Britain's railways were nationalised.

Opposite: In BR days, 2–6–2 tanks handled much of the traffic on the branches radiating from Taunton. These locos came in two basic sizes – large and small – though there were detailed variations. No. 4160 seen in the previous photograph is an example of what is commonly known as a large Prairie – Prairie being the nomenclature for a 2–6–2 wheel arrangement. In contrast, a small Prairie was photographed in March 1997 between Stogumber and Crowcombe Heathfield with a train for Bishops Lydeard.

Small Prairie no. 4561 leaves Watchet with a train for Minehead in March 1997. She was built at Swindon in 1924 and withdrawn in 1962. From the Taunton direction, the approach to Watchet is the first place where one sees the sea. I can still recall the thrill of that first glimpse as a child, even if the tide was out.

5

The 1990s
Steam in all Five Continents: Part 2

Cuba as a steam destination had not really crossed my mind until an article appeared in a magazine accompanied by some stunning pictures. It was clear an abundance of steam locos could be seen during the sugar harvest, the *zafra,* and that despite the sub-editor's groan-inducing headline 'Cuban Sugar Puffs' there was some serious locomotive work to be experienced. One publication in the mid-1990s listed 63 mills with a total of 301 steam locos of which 225 were standard gauge and 76 narrow. The vast majority of engines were of US extraction. Their survival was due in part to the lack of foreign exchange and in part to the US trade embargo.

One of the first mills visited on a trip in 1995 was Pablo de la Torriente Brau, in the western part of the island. Standard gauge 2–6–0 no. 1102 was built for this mill in 1915 by the Vulcan Iron Works, USA. She was photographed in February 1995 leaving one of the loading points in the cane fields. The black smoke had not been requested in advance. No. 1102 was genuinely struggling to find her feet. With its steep gradients and severe curves, the Pablo system provided some spectacular sights.

No. 1102 (left) was seen again later shunting the mill yard in company with no. 1703, another 2–6–0.
Unusually for Cuba, the latter was of German origin, having been supplied by Henschel in 1920.

At Juan Ávila mill in March
1995, no. 1720 passes a
stand of palm trees on the
approach to the yards. She
was a standard gauge 2–6–0
built in the USA by the
Vulcan Iron Works in 1920.
The numberplate on the
front of the smokebox was
presumably for the benefit
of short-sighted train-
spotters.

Looking through the lists of Cuban steam, one is struck by the number of locos built in the 1910s and 1920s. There must have been a big expansion of the sugar industry during that period, although many mills later acquired cast-offs from the national rail network. 2–8–0 no. 1625 is another 1920 standard gauge product, this time from the American builders, Baldwin. She was photographed shunting the yard at Antonio Sánchez mill in March 1995.

Like China, Cuba was a country which at the time of my first visit was not well known to Brits. Back home, people wanted to know what it was like. Friendly is the overriding impression one came away with – surprising really, when one considers how little Cubans have in the way of the material possessions we take for granted. Life in the hotels catering for Western tourists must seem the height of luxury to the average Cuban. In the 1990s, American dollars gave tourists privileged access to goods and services – ironic in the light of the US embargo. There were even petrol stations which took only dollars. Such was the authorities' desire to attract foreign earnings that 'lady escorts' touting for clients in and around tourist hotels were openly tolerated.

What else? The faded glory of old Havana. American automobiles. Cocktails. Cigars. Music. Above all, the relaxed pace of life.

Without a shadow of doubt, the most scenic of Cuban sugar lines were those at Rafael Freyre mill towards the eastern end of the island. Here one could watch 2ft 6in gauge Baldwin 2–8–0s hauling rakes of loaded cane through lush tropical countryside. The length of some of the trains was amazing given the gauge, the relative size of the locos and the gradients. On some of the steepest parts of the line, it was not uncommon for a train to take two or three goes to get to the top of the climb. At other times, it was necessary to detach a few wagons at the foot of the hill. The sight and sound of these diminutive Baldwins at the limits of their capability were something to behold and to enjoy.

If there was a downside, it was the unpredictability of the loco workings and of the climate. Many trains ran after dark. Locos usually worked tender-first on outward-bound empties. And there was the rain. Tropical thunderstorms may not last very long but they are capable of delivering a heck of an amount of water. All of this meant that trying to chase trains by car over dirt roads was something of an adventure. I well remember failing to clear a mud-hole and grounding the car. As a result, four of us had to lever it out. Ironically, this was on a day when no trains were running because heavy rain had made the sugar cane too wet to mill. Of such experiences are memories made.

No. 1390 was built for this mill in 1912 and came from the Baldwin Locomotive Works in Philadelphia, USA. She heads a rake of empties near Bariay in March 1995.

No. 1390 again, near Paraiso (above). Some of the passengers on the tender were probably locals hitching a ride to one of the small communities alongside the railway. Dumped locos do nothing for me, but the slogans on no. 1405 (right) made for a photograph with a difference. In March 1995 the 3ft gauge system at Augusto César Sandino mill looked derelict. Remarkably, visitors the following year found the mill in operation with many of the locos overhauled. Such is the unpredictability of industrial steam. No. 1405 was supplied to Cuba by the German firm Henschel in 1913.

The lack of certainty as to the attitude of the powers-that-be towards camera-toting gricers made Cuba one of those places best visited in a group. One of the leaders in this field was the Dorridge Travel Service whose director David Ibbotson specialised in tours to Latin and South America. An obituary to David in the *Continental Railway Journal* in early 2011 remarked: 'His ability both to plan trips and to sort out the many things that go wrong on the day was amazing.' One's gratitude to David and to other group operators like him is readily acknowledged. Without them, I doubt my photographic collection would be as geographically extensive.

One of the less familiar Dorridge destinations was Sri Lanka. Steam there finished in the 1970s, but by some good fortune, a few locos escaped being cut up and were eventually restored. In 1986 the first steam-hauled tourist train ran under the name 'Viceroy Special'.

In February 1994, the 'Viceroy Special' pauses at Watawala. Heading the train is 4–6–0 no. 340 *Frederick North*. She was built in Darlington by the firm of Robert Stephenson & Hawthorn in the mid-1940s. The second loco is no. 213, a 4–6–0 tender tank constructed by the Vulcan Foundry at Newton-le-Willows in 1922. If the distance between the rails looks wide, that's because it is – 5ft 6in, the same as India's broad gauge.

No. 340 makes a false start from Gampola en route from Kandy to Hatton. Venturing into lineside vegetation has its own hazards – in this case leeches. Ouch!

China hadn't really grabbed me on my first visit in 1982. As I wrote in *Steam Railways Around the World*: 'Somehow, the realisation didn't match the expectation. Yes, the Great Wall is impressive . . . and there is nothing quite like the Terracotta Army near Xian. But despite its cultural heritage, China seemed drab and dull.' I was certainly in no hurry to go back.

Yet as the country opened up to foreigners and more and more enthusiasts visited, it became obvious just how much steam there was to see. Putting qualms to one side, I knew I had to catch some of the action before it was too late. Just one more time? Some hope. I was hooked. A 1996 trip was followed by another a year later and six more in the new millennium.

In the mid-1990s, the star turn on the secondary mainline running from Chifeng to Yebaishou was the morning coal train from Pingzhuang seen here approaching the summit of the line hauled by two unidentified QJs in November 1996. It was sights like this which convinced me to return.

Opposite: For afternoon trains travelling in the opposite direction, there was a superb vantage point on the approach to the tunnel between Shina and Shahai. In November 1996 another unidentified QJ (both images) was photographed with a rake of coal empties bound for Pingzhuang.

In this part of China, when the wind is from the north it comes straight from Siberia. There are stories of camera mechanisms seizing up and some photographers have told of being unable to press the shutter button because of numbness in their fingers. Wind-blown sand and grit can be another problem. More than one film of mine has been scratched by dirt. There's one outstanding memory of the cold from this particular trip. During our stay at Yebaishou, we had the use of a local bus for linesiding and for generally getting around. It was unheated. That wasn't too much of a problem in the daytime. But one evening the driver, having taken us to the local restaurant, decided to wash the floor of the bus before picking us up again. Result – an aisle like a skating rink. I seem to remember the restaurant was none too warm either. I'm sure we kept our coats on throughout the meal.

Of course, there was a good reason why gricers visited China in the winter – the possibility of magnificent photogenic steam effects. However, windless days were rare. More often than not the wind thwarted a perfect shot. On the line from Fuxin to Yebaishou, the exhaust from an unidentified QJ casts a shadow over the loco's tender as it heads a freight towards the summit between Bolouchi and Gongyingzi in November 1996.

The JiTong railway was constructed in the early 1990s and opened for traffic at the end of 1995. Taking its name from the towns at the two ends of the line – Jining and Tongliao – it runs some 600 miles west to east across Inner Mongolia. It seems incredible that the line was built to be worked by steam but this was in fact the case and until 2000 there wasn't a diesel to be seen. From that year onwards, however, diesels began to make inroads until steam was finally eliminated in 2005. It didn't take long for the outside world to hear of this remarkable railway. A French enthusiast is credited for 'discovering' the most celebrated section known as the Jingpeng Pass where the line traverses a gap through the mountains. Virtually all trains over the pass were doubled-headed. This was the place to witness steam power at maximum effort; and the railway soon became the new Mecca for photographers.

In the late 1990s, the only hotels in the Jingpeng area were in Reshui, a small town to the east of the pass. Known to the locals for its hot mineral springs, Reshui had probably never seen Western visitors until the coming of the JiTong railway. The hotels were an interesting experience. In ours, hot bath water (smelling strongly of sulphur) was only available for an hour each evening – 7 to 8 on one floor, 8 to 9 on the next. Meat came on the hoof. One morning, two sheep were tethered outside the kitchen. They weren't there in the evening. No prizes for guessing what was for dinner. Yet despite the remoteness of the region, it was possible to make a direct phone call to the UK.

The curved viaduct at Si Mingyi on the climb from the west was probably the most-frequented lineside location on the pass. If the sun was out, it was almost impossible not to get a good shot of an ascending train. Two unidentified QJs lift a train in October 1997. Seven years later, I rode the footplate of the leading QJ on just such a train – an ear-shattering experience especially inside the four tunnels on the way to the summit.

In a display of maximum effort on the eastern side of the pass, two QJs were photographed negotiating the 180-degree curve at San Di in October 1997.

The station at Shangdian was a passing place just west of the summit tunnel. Here locos often took a breather while waiting to cross trains in the opposite direction, as happened on this occasion in October 1997. For a few dollars, the stationmaster sold me his railway cap.

Two QJs tackle the last part of the climb to the eastern portal of the summit tunnel.

At the end of 1998, my wife and I spent the Christmas holiday period in India. Surely we could escape the commercial trappings and hype which now dominate celebrations in the UK? The appearance of Santa Claus in Jaipur proved otherwise. Happily, dancing round a coal brazier on the terrace of our hotel in Darjeeling under a crystal clear sky on New Year's Eve provided a very different experience. Even more memorably, on the first day of 1999 we were able to lineside the morning train from Kurseong to Darjeeling on the famous 2ft gauge Darjeeling Himalayan Railway (DHR), courtesy of local guide Nima and his jeep named *Midnight Cowboy*.

It's a long, steep and tortuous climb from the plains at Siliguri to the summit of the DHR at Ghum. The railway rises 7,000ft in a little under 50 miles before dropping down into Darjeeling. Sadly, the steam locos are showing their age, and despite tender loving care are limited in the number of carriages they can pull. Today diesels are in charge of the through trains to and from Darjeeling, landslides and washouts permitting; but in 1999 the DHR was still a 100 per cent steam railway.

No. 788 was photographed in the woods below Jor Bungalow. She was a North British Locomotive Co. product of 1913. She had a crew of four – driver, fireman, someone in the bunker atop the boiler breaking coal into manageable pieces, and a man riding at the front whose job it was to sand the rails. The coalman is just visible behind the loco's dome.

6

Into the 21st Century: Cuba & Europe

This book assumes the year 2000 as the first of the new decade. Who now remembers the threat of the Millennium Bug? Anything with a computer chip was supposed to be at risk of malfunction. Was this just a crafty ploy by the IT industry to persuade us all to replace our software? Whatever the truth, the vintage steam locos still at work in Cuba had no such worries. Thanks to Uncle Joe's embargo, there was still a lot of steam activity during the sugar harvest. It really was amazing that at the start of the new century so many steam locos were at work in the backyard of the country with the world's most developed economy.

On the other hand, Cuban steam faced an uncertain future. It seemed that the country was producing more sugar than it could sell on world markets and that in lieu the regime was keen to develop mass tourism as its main income. For how many more years the annual steam bonanza would take place was anyone's guess. In the event, the answer was not many, for in 2003 the *Continental Railway Journal* reported the closure of almost half of the island's mills. This and the consequent transfer of diesels to mills still open had a drastic effect on steam workings. In the words of the *Journal*: 'For seekers after steam operations, the 2003 sugar season can be summed up in two words – game over.' In view of the uncertain prospects, it was time to pay a second visit to Cuba, again with Dorridge Travel Service.

Cubans are proud of their country, hence the hand-painted national flag applied as decoration to a steam loco.

First stop in March 2000 was Rafael Freyre mill where getting around the dirt roads was made easier this time by the use of 4 x 4s rather than ordinary cars and by the absence of thunderstorms. The mainline extended eastwards from the mill for 15 miles with a number of branches serving the various loading points. For the locos hauling trains of cane from the far end, the climb from Progreso to Altuna was a tremendous thrash. Sometimes the rake of loaded wagons was divided into two portions at the foot of the incline, the loco returning to collect the second after having successfully reached the top with the first. Under a sky threatening rain, no. 1387 (no. 5 when supplied new to the mill in 1905) storms the hill in March 2000 (above). The previous day, she was seen (left) taking water at Altuna prior to descending the hill with empties.

Opposite, top: Maximum effort is evident in the photograph of an unidentified Baldwin nearing the mill at Rafael Freyre with a full load of sugar cane in March 2000.

Opposite, bottom: On the line to the mill from the north-west, 2–8–0 no. 1388 was photographed near La Esperanza with a full load of sugar cane. She was built by Baldwin in 1907.

After the 1959 revolution which brought Fidel Castro to power, the sugar industry was nationalised and the mills renamed. Many of the new names were those of political heroes, significant dates or other countries, none of which explains Mal Tiempo, which translates as 'bad weather'. The 2ft 6in gauge system here was a favourite with visiting gricers. Although the countryside through which the railway ran was not particularly hilly, the diminutive Baldwin 2–8–0s had to work flat out over the many ups and downs. One curious feature was the earth tremors which preceded an approaching train. The oil burners in the fireboxes of the locos were positioned very near ground level. When going full blast, they produced shock waves which could be felt and heard some way in advance – strange but true. The drumming also threw up a lot of dust from the ground which was a bit of a nuisance from a photographic point of view. The dust, if not the vibrations, is evident in this photograph of no. 1355 with a loaded train attacking one of the gradients in March 2000. She was a 2–8–0 built by Baldwin in 1920.

Above: No. 1355 crosses the Rio La Virga.

Right: Lunch break at Potrelillo, the loading point furthest from Mal Tiempo mill.

Gregorio Arlee Manalich, named after a pre-Revolution martyr, was one of the last Cuban mills to use steam locos. In its heyday it was much visited by enthusiasts, partly because of its proximity to Havana and partly because it had steam on two gauges – standard and 2ft 6in. There was always something going on in the mill precincts. In this March 2000 scene, no. 1306 backs a rake of loaded wagons into the mill. She was another Baldwin 2–8–0, this time of 1912 vintage.

For readers who may be interested in the photographic equipment used in my travels, it's time to mention changes in cameras round about this time. From 1981 to the mid-1990s, all my work was with a Pentax Spotmatic F SLR camera acquired second-hand from a friend who had purchased it new in 1974. Towards the end of the decade, components started to fail owing to wear and tear – and most probably Chinese grit. To replace it, I bought a Nikon manual SLR but soon came to the conclusion that the quality of the lens was not a patch on that of the Pentax. As luck would have it, I had the chance to buy another Spotmatic F which had hardly ever been used. It was still in its original box complete with instruction booklet. What a find! It's now my camera of choice though I occasionally use the Nikon as a back-up, and I have just acquired a pocket digital camera for fun pictures. Ilford XP2 is my preferred film for black and white photography. When Ilford went bust, the American firm Harman bought the rights to manufacture Ilford film products. A recent article in the national press quoted Harman as saying sales of 35mm film had increased because of a renewed interest in traditional cameras and the challenge of mastering traditional photographic techniques. Fancy that.

Yet another 2ft 6in gauge system could be found at Espartaco mill. In March 2000, no. 1328 backs slowly through the yards. With a 2–8–0 wheel arrangement, she was built by Baldwin in 1915.

As a final look at Cuban steam, here are two standard gauge shed scenes from March 2000. Contrary to appearances, no. 1732 (above) is the older of these two locos. She was built in the Schenectady workshops of the American Locomotive Co. in 1916, originally for mainline use. A 4–6–0, she was being prepared at Orlando González Ramirez mill prior to her day's work. No. 1804 (below) was a Baldwin 2–8–0 and is the junior by three years. She was photographed outside the sheds at Amistad con los Pueblos mill.

Goodbye Cuba. Hello Hungary. As I have explained elsewhere, railway authorities in some parts of the world are willing to cooperate with specialist groups to re-create the steam scene of yesteryear – at a price. Led by David Rodgers, the organisation Steam Loco Safari Tours (SLST) was a specialist in this field. David went to considerable lengths to ensure the 'right' locomotive was used on the 'right' stock over the 'right' route, i.e. an engine on a line over which it would have worked in the 1950s, '60s or whenever with carriages or freight wagons authentic for the period concerned.

The SLST tour of Hungary in 2001 is in my top three group trips. The fact that David had been to Hungary to find the best photo stops was an indication of how well the tour had been planned. On only one occasion was the chosen locomotive facing the wrong way. Mind, the weather helped. There was full sun for the whole of the nine days. The only rain we saw was at Budapest airport while we were waiting for the flight home.

To get a flavour of the trip, it's worth quoting from the advance notes: 'The tour aims to make use of a wide selection of steam locomotives hauling interesting historic and authentic passenger and freight rolling stock, plus two narrow gauge charters . . . there will be some free time to visit side attractions and for general tourism.' An evening boat trip on the Danube got the tour off to a good start, especially as there was free wine. Steam enthusiasts can usually make time for a drink or two.

The depot at Budapest North was at one time the largest in Eastern Europe with an allocation of 200 locos. It is now a museum. In April 2001, 2–8–0 no. 411.118 was specially steamed for the benefit of the SLST group. Over 2,000 class S-160 2–8–0s were built in the USA between 1942 and 1954 for shipment to Europe. No. 411.118 was a Baldwin product of 1944. She was one of a large number of surplus locos purchased by the Hungarian state railways after the Second World War.

Hungary was able to provide an authentic nineteenth-century train. This comprised three historic four-wheel passenger coaches hauled by 4–4–0 no. 204. Built in Budapest in 1900, she is the sole survivor of a class of 200 locos constructed between 1881 and 1905 for express passenger work. Withdrawn in 1952, she was restored to working order in 1988.

In May 2001, no. 204 was photographed near Dunaalmás. Behind the trees is the River Danube. It proved extraordinarily difficult to take a photograph of the train with the river in the background. However, this feat was accomplished with another train later in the day – see page 77 of *Worldwide Steam Railways*.

Our hotel that evening was at Esztergom, an old town on the southern bank of the Danube which had been the seat of the Hungarian monarchs from the tenth to the thirteenth centuries. 'Would we like a wine tasting session before dinner?' asked the local guide. 'Is the Pope Catholic?' – an appropriate response given that the head of the Roman Catholic Church in Hungary has his official residence at Esztergom. What better way to end a successful day's gricing?

No. 204 again, this time making a false start from Neszmély. An explanation of run-pasts and false starts has been given in an earlier chapter. On group tours, there's usually at least one person who keeps meticulous notes – and it's not me. Someone else calculated that during nine days of steam photography in Hungary, 133 run-pasts and false starts were achieved. Not bad, though this figure didn't reach that of the Drakensberg Farewell Tour referred to in chapter 3.

Instead of a false start, here's a false arrival. Class 424 4–8–0 no. 424.247 arrives at Pásztó in May 2001 with a freight train en route to Hatvan. She's an oil-burner, which may account for the ready-made black smoke. The advance notes for the Hungary tour described this class as the country's finest steam loco design. Over 500 were built for mixed traffic work between 1924 and 1958, no. 424.247 being delivered in 1955. The signals look very foreign to British eyes.

No. 424.009 (above) is a member of the same class, though from appearances one could be forgiven for thinking otherwise. A coal-burner, she hails from the first year of production, and was photographed at Dorog bound for Budapest. The high-pitched boiler is very distinctive and gives the loco a towering look.

By contrast, no. 394.057 (right) seems almost petite. She was photographed at Szalajkavolgy in May 2001 on a narrow gauge line which is a remnant of a former forestry railway. With an 0–6–0 wheel arrangement, this class of loco was used on light agricultural and industrial lines. No. 394.057 was built in 1949.

This page and the next depict a contrast in passenger trains. Pictured above is a re-creation of a typical branch line scene from the steam era, though the coaches wouldn't have looked so spick and span. Between 1907 and 1959 – the last year of Hungarian steam production – over 700 class 375 2–6–2 tank locos were built. No. 375.562, seen here in action near Eplény in May 2001, was constructed in 1923.

An outstanding feature of the SLST tour of Hungary was the use (for two consecutive nights) of the coaches which form the 'Royal Hungarian Express', a luxury train aimed at wealthy tourists. Used by senior party leaders in Communist days, the train included the Presidential sleeping car and dining car, all restored to their original livery and panelled internally with mahogany. Dinner was as sumptuous as one could wish for on a train. Particularly memorable was the aperitif – Hungary's famous Tokaji wine – drunk in the splendour of the dining car whilst gliding along the northern shore of Lake Balaton. Not all steam tours are an endurance test. To reinforce the point, the next evening's meal was taken in wine cellars at Eger, a town in the north-east of the country and the centre of another viniculture region.

During the first day aboard this luxury train, we were hauled by class 109 4–6–0 no. 109 photographed between Boba and Sumeg. To understand this loco's origins requires a short history lesson. Prior to its dismemberment at the end of the First World War, the Austro-Hungarian Empire included part of what is now Italy and much of the Balkans. The Austrian Southern Railway, the *Südbahn*, was created in order to link Vienna with the Adriatic city of Trieste, the empire's major port. From 1910 to 1914, 44 class 109 locos were built to work the principal expresses on this route. However, the *Südbahn* also operated a network of tracks running eastwards into Hungary, thus joining the empire's two capital cities, Vienna and Budapest, by rail. Ten more of the class were constructed between 1914 and 1917 for these Hungarian lines. When the empire was split up after the war, the allocation of the original 44 locos was divided between Austria, Italy and Yugoslavia. The later ten remained in Hungary. No. 109 was built by the Austrian manufacturer Florisdorf in Vienna in 1917. Painted apple green with red frame and wheels, she is a most handsome machine.

2–6–2 no. 324.540 was photographed on a mixed train in May 2001 leaving Zirc (above) and near Vinye (below). Built in 1915, she was a survivor from a class of over 900 locos whose construction started in 1909 and continued into the 1940s.

Another year, another country. So impressive had been SLST's performance in Hungary that I decided to join its tour to the Czech Republic in the following year. A holiday in 1995 had been timed to coincide with a special weekend of steam activity in Prague and had whetted the appetite for more.

Railway photography in Czechoslovakia during the Communist era was a bit of a hit-and-miss affair. Sometimes the authorities appeared relaxed. At other times, the opposite was only too true, even to the extent of revoking permissions previously granted at short notice and with no explanation. Despite this, Czech steam attracted many gricers, in part because of the mix of ancient and modern motive power. Czechoslovakia was created from the break-up of the Austro-Hungarian Empire at the end of the First World War. The state railways thus found themselves with locos of almost 200 different classes from the two constituent parts of the empire as well as from the many private railways which had been absorbed. Some standardisation took place in the 1920s and '30s but events during the Second World War led to much stock being lost to Germany and its ally Hungary. Consequently, the late 1940s and early '50s saw the introduction of new classes incorporating the latest technical developments, though locos from the *ancien régime* were still at work in the 1960s.

One of the first new designs was the class 498 4–8–2s, of which no. 498.022, built by Skoda in 1946, was photographed in October 2002 between Horny Cerekov and Hribeci.

The class 556 locos have been regarded by some experts as the ultimate European heavy freight design. Incorporating features from contemporary steam locomotive developments in France and Germany, 510 engines of these 2–10–0s were constructed by Škoda between 1951 and 1958, the last proving to be the final steam loco delivered to the Czech railways. No. 556.0506 was built in 1957 and had the sad task in 1981 of working the last steam-hauled passenger train on the state railways. She was photographed in October 2002 arriving at Nové Hrady (above) with a charter freight from České Budejovice to České Velenice, and near Petrikov on the return journey (below). What a magnificent machine.

One of the most distinctive of the post-war Czech designs was the class 477 4–8–4 tank locomotives, of which sixty were delivered to the state railways between 1951 and 1955. With their high-pitched boilers, these machines had a very impressive appearance enhanced by the livery of light blue and red wheels. No. 477.043 is of 1954 vintage and was photographed waiting to leave Beroun (above) in October 2002 with a passenger train to Rakovnik.

The 600mm gauge Mladejov industrial railway is situated in the east of the Czech Republic. Built to transport minerals, it twists and climbs for 7 miles through attractive hilly wooded countryside to Hrebec. On what is now a museum operation, it is possible to re-create the past with steam-hauled trains of side-tipper wagons. 0–6–0+2 Engerth-type locos 1 and 5 (right) double-head a train out of the yards at Mladejov, the lower terminus, in October 2004. No. 1 of Emett-like appearance was built by Krauss in 1920 for the opening of the railway. No. 5 followed from the same manufacturer nine years later.

As recounted in *Worldwide Steam Railways*, Jindřichův Hradec is the terminus of two 760mm gauge lines which since 1998 have been run by a private company. Regular traffic is worked by diesels but steam is used for special occasions as in October 2004 when 0–6–2 no. U37.002 worked a SLST charter to the northern end of the line at Obratan where she is seen (above) arriving in the early evening. An action replay enabled the 'artistic' shot (below) to be attempted as the train crossed a bridge. Appreciation of this type of composition depends on one's taste, and to be honest I'm not sure it's mine. This loco was built in Linz, Austria, by the firm of Krauss in 1898. That made her 106 years old at the time of the photograph.

The charm of the narrow gauge is a hackneyed phrase, but apposite to this photograph of no. U37.002 rolling into the station at Včelnička in October 2004

Neighbouring Austria has a number of narrow gauge lines which regularly see steam. The Zillertalbahn follows the valley of the River Ziller from Jenbach, a station on the mainline from Innsbruck to Salzburg, to the winter sports centre of Mayrhofen. This is an everyday railway with a year-round service of diesel passenger trains. In the summer and at other holiday times, there are steam trains primarily for the tourist market. A ride on a steam train on Christmas Day is only possible in places like Austria where the day is regarded as an opportunity for a family outing. Trains run, ski resorts are in full swing and restaurants open, family and religious celebrations having taken place on the evening of Christmas Eve.

There is nothing special about the photograph above, taken in 2002, other than as a record of the only steam journey I have taken on a Christmas Day. That said, the loco is of interest. Built in Linz by Krauss in 1909, it is an 0–8–2 which formerly saw service in Yugoslavia where it was numbered 83.076. Owned by an Austrian preservation group who acquired the loco from Bosnia-Herzegovina, it was on loan to the Zillertalbahn where it carried the number 4. Heading a train of eighteen packed coaches, she was photographed at one of the intermediate stations en route to Mayrhofen (above) and later running round at the terminus (left).

The Waldviertalbahn is a 760mm gauge system in the north of Austria close to the Czech border. Starting from the town of Gmund, the original line north to Litschau with a branch to Heidenreichstein was opened in 1900. A few years later, another route was constructed south from Gmünd to Groß Gerungs. Passenger services on the northern lines were scrapped in 1986, thus ending the opportunity of photographing simultaneous parallel steam departures from the junction at Alt Nagelberg, a well-known feature of the operations. At the same time, diesel railcars were introduced on the line to Groß Gerungs. However, they failed to halt the decline in passenger numbers, and the system closed not long after celebrating its centenary. Until 1997 steam was still occasionally used for freight traffic, which was chiefly of timber, and for passenger trains on high days and holidays.

The southern section is particularly attractive running at first through open countryside and then through densely wooded hills. The twists and turns and the steep gradients make for serious work on the part of the locomotives; and in recent times, steam-hauled trains were in the hands of a few powerful 0–8+4 locos of the Engerth type. Invented by Wilhelm von Engerth in the 1850s for use on the railway then being constructed over the Semmering Pass in the Austrian Alps, this was a design whereby the tender was articulated with the main locomotive frame so that some of the weight of the coal and water was carried by the driving wheels, thus improving adhesion while still allowing the loco to negotiate sharp curves.

No. 399.04 was one of six narrow gauge Engerth locos supplied by Krauss to another Austrian railway, the Mariazellerbahn, four in 1906 and two more in 1908. When that line was later electrified, all six were transferred to the Waldviertalbahn. In October 2004 only no. 399.04 was in working order and is seen below at Weitra with a SLST charter.

Another interesting feature of the Waldviertalbahn was that the current terminus at Gmünd was not the original starting point. That was in the town of Česke Velenice which after the First World War found itself in newly created Czechoslovakia. It wasn't until the 1920s that the present terminus at Gmünd was provided. Even then, trains on the northern route still had to pass through Czech territory. But with the USSR's domination of Eastern Europe after the Second World War came the Iron Curtain; and in 1950 a short diversion was constructed so that trains remained on Austrian territory. In October 2004 no. 399.04 was photographed on the northern line with a SLST charter bound for Heidenreichstein.

As already mentioned, my first visit to the Czech Republic was not long after the fall of the Iron Curtain. After a few days in Prague, my wife and I spent a week's holiday on a farm in the south of the country. With a hired car – yes, a Škoda – we were able to enjoy the unspoilt countryside of Bohemia. One day we drove across the border to Gmünd in order to ride the regular Saturdays and Sundays steam train to Groß Gerungs. Three things stick in the memory. First, the ease of the border crossing compared to the experience in the bad old days. So paranoid and restrictive was the Communist regime that many country roads in areas of Czechoslovakia bordering Austria and Germany could be used only by locals holding special permits. Almost the sole remaining visual evidence of those days was the occasional derelict watch-tower. It transpired that since the fall of the barriers, some of these roads had been turned into cycle tracks and that car use was still restricted to the local populace. Happily, no one told us and we couldn't read the road signs. Second, a coach party aboard the train complete with an oompah band. The high spirits, fuelled no doubt by copious amounts of beer, confounded one's stereotypical image of the staid Austrian, and kept my wife amused while I disappeared to ride on the open balcony of the coaches, the better to enjoy the third abiding image – that of the steam loco blasting its way through hills and woods.

Memories of that holiday are revived by no. 399-04 entering the station at Alt Weitra with a train from Gmünd to Weitra in October 2004.

The Ybbstalbahn was yet another Austrian 760mm gauge line which saw occasional steam trains thanks to the efforts of preservation groups, one of which owned U class 0–6–4 tank no. 598.02. She was built by Krauss as long ago as 1896 but showed no sign of her age in October 2004 when SLST chartered a mixed train over the 50 or so miles from Waidhofen, the junction with the standard gauge, to the then terminus for regular service trains at Lunz am See. Most of the route followed the valley of the River Ybbs through typical Alpine scenery. No carriages from the steam era have survived, so one had to make do with a modern coach. Some timber wagons were added to provide a measure of authenticity.

In this pastoral scene, 598.02 ambles through the meadows near Oisberg. What a delightful way to spend a crisp autumn day. Warm sunshine. Clear blue skies. The first tinges of yellow and gold on the trees. No people and no cars. Just the gentle purr of a steam loco on a country branch line. An abundance of run-pasts or false arrivals. Lunch of beer and home-made goulash in a village *gasthof*. Perfect.

In Poland a few narrow gauge lines managed to survive into the twenty-first century. One of these was the remnant of a network emanating from the town of Gniezno which at its peak had a trackage of some 50 miles. In 2001 it still carried freight and there were moves to develop the line as a tourist attraction. Best of all, it was possible to re-create a passenger train of yesteryear by hiring one's own train and, once out of the town precincts, to drive it. With no other traffic on the line, run-pasts could be arranged as many times as one wanted.

Class Px48 0–8–0 no. 1785 is an example of the standard design developed by the Polish state railways for their narrow gauge lines after the Second World War. Above, she is performing a run-past with the 'Strickland Special' en route to Witkowo in October 2001. A conveniently placed haystack provided a good vantage point. Below, she storms through a roadside village with a Brit at the controls. The track at this point was so overgrown as to make the rails almost invisible.

Dresden is a convenient base for exploring the steam narrow gauge lines which have survived in Saxony. Four all-year-round operations are within striking distance. Moreover, each connects with the main railways and can therefore easily be reached from the city by train.

The survival of these lines is due in large measure to the relatively low standard of living in the Communist era. Private car ownership was for the few. Public transport was therefore much used not just for getting to work but also for family outings. As one author has remarked, people were allowed to enjoy themselves even if they were being spied upon while doing so. That said, the state railways were keen to divest themselves of their narrow gauge operations as soon as practicable after unification of East and West Germany; and those that remain are run by private companies.

Zittau in the far south-eastern corner of Saxony, very near the Polish border, is the starting point for a 750mm gauge line running into the hilly countryside south of the town and much patronised by hikers. For the railway enthusiast there is the added attraction of parallel steam departures from the intermediate station of Bertsdorf where the route splits into two branches. Sadly, at the time of my one and only visit, hopes of photographing this spectacle were dashed – one of the branches had been closed for maintenance and trains replaced by buses. Shades of UK weekends.

2–10–2 tank no. 99.731 crosses the entrance to Zittau's mainline station with the stock of a train for Kurort Oybin in April 2002. This class of locomotive was much used on the Saxon narrow gauge lines. Thirty-two were built between 1928 and 1933 and a further twenty-four between 1952 and 1956.

The 10 mile-long line from Radebeul to Radeburg starts in the suburbs of Dresden but soon reaches open countryside. The first crossing station is Friedewald where, in October 2004, no. 99.713 was photographed (right) arriving with a train to Radeburg. Later she was seen again near Barnsdorf (below). An 0–10–0, this loco was built by the firm of Hartmann in 1927.

One narrow gauge line which didn't make it to unification was that from Wolkenstein to Johstadt. Closed in 1986 by Deutsche Reichsbahn (DR), the state railways of the German Democratic Republic (East Germany), a 5-mile section is operated by a preservation group under the title Pressnitztalbahn. Locomotives, rolling stock and stations have been restored to a very high standard. For some observers, this is as authentic a re-creation of the past as one could hope for. Add the attractive wooded valley through which the line runs and a visit to Johstadt is a must.

In October 2004, the Pressnitztalbahn had another locomotive of the same class as that seen in the previous two photographs. Carrying the number 99.1715 and with an 0–10–0 wheel arrangement, this loco belonged to a class which had its origins in the First World War where it was used by military railways on the German side. At the end of the war some were transferred to the Saxon State Railways and more were built in the 1920s.

In DR days, the railway from Wolkenstein to Johstadt was famous for its 0–4–4–0 tanks. Known as Saxon-Meyers, they were an articulated loco designed for hilly curved branch lines. Ninety-six were built by Hartmann between 1892 and 1921. Three have been preserved in working order on the Pressnitztalbahn where no. 99.1590 was photographed double-heading with no. 99.1715 on the approach to Schmalzgrube with a goods train. The two vintage motor coaches just happened to appear. Germany has bus enthusiasts, too.

No. 99.1590 waits to leave Steinbach with a passenger train for Johstadt in October 2004. I think the building behind the loco houses a water tower.

On many continental narrow gauge lines, transporter wagons were used on which standard gauge freight trucks could be carried piggy-back. Some were included in this goods train on the Pressnitztalbahn seen leaving Schmalzgrube behind no. 99.1715, also in October 2004.

Another museum operation can be found at Weißwasser, north-east of Dresden, hard
against the Polish border. Known as the Waldeisenbahn Muskau, it is an extensive
600mm gauge network of lines originally built to serve sawmills and lignite mines on
the estate of a local squire. Subsequently taken over by DR, it continued to function as
an industrial railway until closure in 1978. Now run as a tourist attraction, it offers the
chance to photograph authentic re-creations of the line's past. A train of coal wagons
leaves Bad Muskau in October 2004. In charge is loco no. 99.3317, an 0–8–0 tank loco
built by the firm of Borsig in 1918.

0–8–0 no. 99.3312 hauls a train of logs from Weißwasser to Muhlrose. Of 1912 vintage, she worked on the railway in DR days. This narrow gauge system is unlike most heritage steam railways. It was never a passenger-carrying line, and it's the freight operations which are the attraction. Being in an un-touristy part of Germany it doesn't get many overseas visitors, which may account for the exceptionally warm welcome which the SLST group received on its visit on October 2004. Nothing was too much trouble. Trains were run on parts of the system not normally used by the public. And the wurst and beer were plentiful and delicious.

Another area of Germany not that well known to Brits is the Baltic Sea coastline of the former Communist part of the country, though it has been much favoured by German holidaymakers ever since the seaside became fashionable under the patronage of the nobility. One such resort is Heiligendamm which in the nineteenth-century grew from a fishing village into a major resort and which in 1886 was linked to the mainline at Bad Doberan by a 900mm gauge railway. Later extended further along the coast to Kühlungsborn, this railway is now privately owned though receiving financial support from the local authorities. Known as the Molli – allegedly after the name of a dog which chased the very first train in 1886 – the line provides a year-round service of steam passenger trains from Bad Doberan to the coast.

Among steam enthusiasts, the line is famous for the street running in Bad Doberan. To ride a steam train as it runs slap bang through the middle of a street of shops is a little out of the ordinary these days, at least in Europe. Equally, there is something very satisfying about lunching on steak and chips as a steam loco passes within feet – or rather metres – of the restaurant's window.

Opposite: Two photographs taken in April 2003 of trains leaving the main shopping street in Bad Doberan. The loco no. 99.2321 is a 2–8–2 tank delivered to the line in 1932 from the works of Orenstein & Koppel.

Further east lies Germany's largest island, Rugen, which at one time had a 750mm gauge network of lines totaling some 60 miles. A part survives primarily providing a service to tourists and holidaymakers. No. 99.4802 is a 2–8–0 Henschel of 1938 vintage which came to Rugen in the mid-1960s from a closed line in another part of East Germany. She is about to depart (above) from the wayside halt at Jagdschloß with a train from Göhren to Putbus. In gricer parlance, this was a grab shot. I had jumped down from the train to take the photo and only just managed to get back on as the loco started to move.

Moving south and eastwards geographically speaking, we come to the Balkans and the countries which collectively made up the former Yugoslavia. Despite the relatively ease of access for Western holidaymakers in the Cold War era, the country was one of the most repressive and authoritarian in its attitude to railway photographers. In the words of one well-known author, this attitude 'made the pursuit of steam a challenging and often futile exercise.' It was only the very determined, or foolhardy, who chanced their arm. Then came the break-up after the fall of Communism and the subsequent strife. Thus it was a long time before it felt OK to venture forth to sample what steam remained. Even then, it was with a group on the safety-in-numbers principle.

One of the most numerous classes of steam loco in Yugoslavia was the class 01 2–6–2 used extensively for passenger traffic. The first six of this class were built by the Berlin firm of Schwarzkopf in 1912. A further 120 were acquired by the Serbian, Croatian and Slovenian Railways in 1922/23 as war reparations from Germany. The class survived into the 1980s, the last five being withdrawn from use in 1985. No. 01-088 is available for charters in Serbia and was photographed (above) in June 2008 near Ruma while working a special train from Loznica to Belgrade. She looked superb in the early evening sun. This is one of the few photographs in this book which has been doctored by computer software to eliminate an unsightly feature, in this case a cable affixed to the pole on the right. In addition to being strung across the sky, it cast a dark shadow along the length of the locomotive.

Staying in Belgrade was an almost surreal experience with the effects of NATO bombing still much in evidence. The relatively recent history of these parts was also forcefully brought home in neighbouring Bosnia-Herzegovina where burned-out houses, shell marks, and signs warning of roadside mines were frequently seen. None of this diminished the welcome we received from the railway workforce.

Bosnia-Herzegovina still has active industrial steam; and at the Banovici coal mines, it can be seen on two gauges – standard and 760mm. Yugoslavia once had a huge network of narrow gauge lines, the classic locomotives of which were the class 83 0–8–2s. In June 2008, no. 83-158 of 1948 vintage was still at work at Banovici (below right). I doubt many impartial observers could explain let alone understand the issues which gave rise to the conflict in the Balkans in the mid-1990s. Religious beliefs no doubt were mixed in somewhere because Bosnia-Herzegovina is one of those areas where Christianity meets Islam. One village has a church; the next a mosque. I failed to make a note of the location (below left) where ex-German 2–10–0 no. 33-236 performed a run-past with a special train from Brcko to Tuzla in June 2008. She normally worked on industrial lines which served the Kreka coal mines near Tuzla.

7

Into the 21st Century: Asia

The Middle East had for a long time been a gap in my search for world steam. This state of affairs was righted in September 2008 by joining a Railway Touring Company (RTC) tour to Syria and Jordan, the major part of which consisted of steam-hauled special trains on the Hedjaz Railway, a line made famous by Lawrence of Arabia's exploits in the First World War.

Our first journey was south from Jordan's capital, Amman. We hadn't gone more than a mile before one of the carriage windows took a direct hit from children who seemed to regard throwing stones at trains as some kind of local sport.

Fortunately there were no troublesome boys to bother us on the hillside overlooking the viaduct in the suburbs of Amman, a location well known to gricers. It wasn't that many years ago that this was an open vista, such has been the speed at which Amman has spread, partly owing to an influx of Iraqi refugees, or so we were told. The high-rise building does nothing to improve the scene. No. 23 was a 2–8–2 constructed by the British firm of Robert Stephenson & Hawthorn in 1951.

Another run-past took place against the backdrop of a mosque with a gleaming golden dome (above). Leaving Amman behind, the train eventually reached a ruined station seemingly in the middle of a desert. In running round, the loco derailed. Don't panic – it's in such situations that it's good to have a leader to do the worrying. Miraculously, the bus taking the group on to Petra managed to find us and all was well. Petra – ah, that was another unforgettable experience as was taking a jeep into Lawrence of Arabia country at Wadi Rum. Before the derailment, a local boy appeared from nowhere to be photographed as no. 23 made a false arrival with the RTC special.

Between Amman and Al Qasir, the railway crosses the main highway running south from the capital. When travelling behind no. 23 I'd spotted the photographic potential here and requested a stop the next time we came this way. So a few days later, no. 71 performed for the photo gallery at the road crossing. No gates or barriers – just a man waving frantically. No. 71 is a 2–8–2 built in Belgium for the Hedjaz-Jordan Railway in 1955 by the firm of Haine St Pierre.

From Jordan the Railway Travel Company party travelled by steam train into Syria. No. 85 of the Jordanian Railways was photographed south of Al Mafraq. She was a Pacific built in Japan in the 1950s.

By rail, the border between Jordan and Syria was invisible. Coming back by road it was a very different story – three hours to clear two sets of customs posts. North of Deraa, the first town on the Syrian side of the border and the scene of pro-democracy protests in 2011, we travelled behind Syrian Railways 2–8–2 no. 262. Built in Germany by Hartmann in 1918, she is seen here waiting for the photographers to return to the train after a run-past somewhere in the middle of nowhere.

And so to Damascus, Syria's capital – a fascinating place. Though Islam is the predominant religion, the city has special significance for Christians. For gricers of whatever faith or none, there is the attraction of the remnant of a line which long ago linked Damascus to Beirut. No. 755, a 2–6–0 tank built in Switzerland for the opening of this railway in 1895, takes a RTC special to Fidjeh in September 2008. Like the Hedjaz Railway, this line has the unusual gauge of 1.05 metres.

At the beginning of the twenty-first century, Burma was an unlikely place to find everyday steam, yet such was the case until all of the remaining operational locomotives were withdrawn at a stroke in April 2008. It was fortunate, therefore, that I decided to join a Railway Touring Company steam tour of Burma in January 2007. Another couple of years and it would have been too late – proof that it sometimes really is the case when I tell my wife that I must go to so-and-so before steam disappears!

But should I have gone? Did a visit imply endorsement of the country's military regime? What about the government's dismal human rights record? Nobody of my acquaintance said much about visiting Communist-era Poland or East Germany, apartheid South Africa, Castro's Cuba, Red China or Mugabe's Zimbabwe. But somehow Burma was a different matter. Why? In 2006 the grandson of U Thant, one time Secretary General of the United Nations, wrote about the damaging effect isolation from the West and the international scene was having on the ordinary people of Burma and argued for more trade, more engagement and 'more tourism in particular'. While acknowledging there was a contrary view, I doubted a one-man boycott would have much effect on the attitude of those in charge of the country's affairs, and so booked my place on the tour. How glad I am that I did. This rates as one of my top three group tours, as much for the cultural experiences, and the friendliness and charming nature of the people, as for the steam.

Burma was once part of the British Empire and for a time was administered from India. Burmese railways are of metre gauge. It's no surprise therefore that the country's remaining steam locomotives were of designs employed on India's metre gauge network. Class YD 2–8–2 no. 970 was photographed in January 2007 near Thephyugon with the Railway Touring Company's special train. Built in 1949 by the Vulcan Foundry at Newton-le-Willows, she was one of a number of locos supplied to Burma to replace stock lost to hostilities in the Second World War.

No. 970 again near Thaton (above) and passing a stupa at Yinnyein (below).

There was much to make this tour so memorable. A ride in a palanquin to view a Buddhist shrine at dawn. A whole day's boat ride drifting down the River Irrawaddy. Did you know that the 'road to Mandalay' in Rudyard Kipling's famous poem is the river? The ruined temples and pagodas at Bagan, some 4,000 of them, one of the world's great archaeological sites. Monks and monasteries. Delicious food – a meeting of Indian, Thai and Chinese cuisines. But above all the escape from mass tourism and the natural courtesy of our hosts.

All tours have their problems. Late running of the trains was a particular difficulty in Burma. On one occasion we had to decamp into a bus in order to get to a hotel before the road to it closed for the night – and the last part of the journey was in the dark in the back of a lorry with planks for seats. A few days later, arrival into Mandalay was by steam as planned, but at some ungodly hour of the night. Having been on the train for forty hours with only basic sleeping and eating accommodation, the ladies of the party were not amused.

No. 964 was from the same batch as no. 970. She was photographed leaving Htonebo on the route from Mandalay to Sedaw. From there, but with diesel haulage, the RTC special train ascended the hills by a series of switchbacks to reach Maymyo. In colonial days, this was a hill-station where government officials could escape the heat of the plains. The British influence is still evident in the architecture, both domestic and ecclesiastical, and the nearby botanical gardens. But instead of black cabs, the taxis are horse-drawn carriages which have the appearance of scaled-down Wells Fargo stagecoaches – bizarre.

No. 970 is seen again between Kyaikto and Thaton. Some purists dislike photographs of moving trains which do not include all of the carriages or wagons, but no apology is offered for the inclusion of this shot which for me captures the power and thrill of steam at speed.

That night's stay was in Moulmein. The next day we took a diesel-hauled train to Thanbyuzayat, the Burmese end of the infamous Death Railway built during the Japanese occupation in the Second World War. There we visited the cemetery maintained by the Commonwealth War Graves Commission – a moving experience. More happily, the guard of the diesel train sold me his red and green flags with teak handles. Now hanging in my study, they are a reminder of Burma and the warmth of the people.

Would I go back? Of course. The call of the East is a bit of a cliché, but there's something special about Burma.

You may be wondering whether special trains count as the real thing for Burma. Well, it was obvious regular steam was hanging on the by the skin of its teeth in 2007. During the RTC tour we saw only two steam-hauled trains apart from our own, both freights. There were no such doubts in China. Real steam has lasted into the second decade of the present century, despite rumours that the authorities planned to abolish it before the 2008 Olympic Games. True, steam had been eliminated by then on the national network, but it could still be found in a few industrial locations.

By the early years of the decade, it was clear that the writing was on the wall even on the Jitong line and its by then famous Jingpeng Pass. In 2004 I joined the Jingpeng Orient Express, a luxury train chartered by the UK tour operator GW Travel on which we slept and ate for ten days. The highlights were the narrow gauge system at Huanan, the Jitong line of course, and the private system of the Teifa

Mining Administration, all of which featured in my *Worldwide Steam Railways*. By then, the Jitong line could boast the world's last steam-hauled regular timetabled long-distance passenger train, seen above during a loco change at Chabuga in March 2004. Elsewhere, the Teifa system was still 100 per cent steam with a fleet of SY 2–6–2s, the most recent of which had been constructed in 1999, and a solitary JS 2–8–2, no. 5029 (left) waiting to leave Diaobingshan with a local passenger train. In addition to coal traffic, the Teifa network saw approximately thirty timetabled passenger trains each day.

At Diaobingshan, the footbridge seen in the previous photograph was a marvellous vantage point from which to watch the comings and goings at the station, and at the next-door loco servicing point where SY no. 0665 was being coaled and watered. She was built in Tangshan locomotive factory in 1973. In the background are two SY-hauled passenger trains.

Jalainur open-cast coal pit has been known to the gricing fraternity for a long time. Situated in the north of China not far from the border with Russia, it was a huge operation with trains zig-zagging down into and up out of the pit twenty-four hours a day. Some of the loaded trains carried the soil and rocks which had been stripped away to get at the coal seams. Others carried the coal itself. At the lower levels, the tracks were constantly being shifted as digging went deeper and deeper. Higher up, the formation was more permanent and included double-track sections with colour light signalling. In October 2007, thirty-five active SYs were seen during two-and-a-half days' photography – quite amazing. It was one of those places where one could put the camera away and just enjoy the experience of constant steam activity. But by golly was it cold, even in October, courtesy of a biting north wind from Siberia which, though ensuring blue skies, kicked up a lot of dust and dirt – cue scratched film. In such climatic conditions, the ubiquitous picnic lunch of pot noodles was essential to keeping oneself warm. Even our local guides stayed in the minibus instead of accompanying us into the pit, 'us' being fellow gricer Richard and myself. It seemed remarkable that we managed to walk down into the pit seemingly without any formal permission. No one challenged us. Now and again there was a friendly wave from the loco crew. Otherwise, there was no acknowledgement of our presence. We could only assume those who worked the pit were used to the sight of 'big-noses' – as the Chinese colloquially refer to Europeans – with cameras.

No. 1192 pushes a rake of side-tipping wagons up one of the zigs, or zags. Given the cold, the most unenviable job was that of the guard who rode in the open at the front of the train, there being no guard's van.

The above photograph was taken about a third of the way down the pit. The hut in the foreground appeared to be some sort of refuge for the guards.

At the top of the pit, on what might be termed ground level, SY no. 1371 was photographed in the exchange sidings with China Rail.

Jixi, in the north-east of China, is the centre of an extensive coal-mining area with a number of 'private' rail systems linked to the national network. This part of China is way off the tourist trail but over the years became something of a Mecca for those of us determined to seek out the last of Chinese steam. The perceived wisdom was that winter was the best time to visit from a photographic point of view because of the guaranteed steam effects. But there were drawbacks – the intense cold and industrial pollution. Together they could make one feel very unpleasant. My second visit to Jixi was planned for November before the worst of the winter cold, but even then on some days the thermometer never rose above -10°C. I soon needed something to soothe a hacking cough, which is how I came to find myself in a Chinese pharmacy buying a syrup made from plants. It certainly helped until the bottle was confiscated before leaving Jixi on a domestic flight to Beijing.

A word about Chinese food. If you're an animal lover, don't ask too many questions. It was once said that the Chinese will eat anything which moves, except bicycles. With a local guide to help, some of the less appetising-sounding dishes – hot poke bum, anyone? – can be avoided. Away from tourist hotels, there's no condescension to Western tastes. This isn't a problem at lunch or dinner time, but breakfasts are another matter. As one author has put it: 'Considering the universal deliciousness of Chinese cuisine, it has always been a mystery . . . how Chinese breakfasts could be so bad. You would think after five thousand years of continuous civilisation they could come up with something a little better than pickled vegetables and rice gruel.' Do remember to pack a jar of instant coffee before leaving the UK. Beijing and Shanghai may have their Starbucks but you won't find a decent cup of coffee in Jixi.

One of the busiest of the 'private' systems in the Jixi area is at Didao where in November 2009 an unidentified SY heads a rake of empty coal wagons.

Elsewhere on the Didao system in November 2009, SY no. 0950 (above) brings a train of loaded wagons into the washery and no. 0407 (below) returns from the power station with empties.

Another busy system in the Jixi area was at Chengzihe. Though due to be electrified, it was still 100 per cent steam at the end of the decade. One of the best places to hear and see locos being thrashed was the steep-curved single-line from Dongchang colliery to Beichang washery where SY no. 1052 was photographed in March 2009 (above). Eight months later, sister loco no. 1058 running in the opposite direction passes fellow photographer Richard (below). The houses on the right seem to demonstrate that the benefits of China's economic miracle have yet to reach the poorer and more remote parts of the country.

The Chengzihe system meets the national rail network at Jixi Xi. In the photograph above, taken in March 2009, an unidentified SY approaches the exchange sidings with a full load of coal. Pinggang colliery is in hilly countryside some way south of Jixi. There in November 2009, SY no. 0804 was photographed under the loading silos (below).

Beipiao was one of the smaller, less well-known and less frequently visited colliery railways. In 2009 it was 100 per cent steam though with a stud of only six SYs. In November, no. 1081 was under repair in the workshops (left) where the shadow cast by the red star caught my eye.

No. 1196 was photographed (below and opposite) heading a coal train from Sanbao to the washery at Beipiao. From the empty wagons at the front, it looks as if coal production that day had not been as high as expected.

At the end of the first decade of the new millennium, China is the last place in the world where steam locomotives can be found in quantity at work on 'real' everyday railways. Amazingly there are still a few daily steam-hauled passenger trains, as on the railway system of the Baiyin Non-Ferrous Metals Company in Gansu Province. This company runs passenger trains from the city of Baiyin to mines at Shenbutong. In the final few miles the line clings to a valley side as it climbs steeply into the hills where copper and other metallic ores are mined. A bluff overlooking the valley makes a superb vantage point from which to watch ascending locos working flat out. During a trip to China in October 2011 to catch the country's last steam, I spent three days in Baiyin and came to this spot every day to witness the spectacle of the afternoon passenger train to Shenbutong. Lit by soft autumnal sun, SY no. 1470 (above) gladdens the heart as she pounds uphill. Such was my enthusiasm for this location that fellow gricer Richard Turkington christened it Keith's Bluff.

Over seventeen days, Richard and I saw fifty active steam locomotives at six industrial locations in various parts of China. Though this was a remarkable figure for 2011, it was evident that steam was on the decline. Diesels had made considerable inroads since our previous visit in 2009 and there were plans to acquire more as soon as the money could be found to buy them. Nevertheless, the inscription (below) on the tender of SY no. 1632 seen at Fushun steelworks records that this loco was overhauled at Sujiatun locomotive workshops as recently as August 2011. Perhaps Chinese steam will last a few more years yet!